STIGMATIZED

STIGMATIZED

A ~~NURSE'S~~ HERO'S JOURNEY

ASHLEY WYNN-GRIMES

For the supporting cast in my story. Each of you played a part in inspiring a lesson. You extended love and through your love, I have been provided the opportunity to grow. Thank you for planting your seeds: Mom, Dad, Charis, Brittany, Domonique, Tamina, Qwan, Paula, Aunt Pat, of course my husband and children.

CONTENTS

PART ONE: STRENGTH   9

PART TWO: THE FOOL   17

PART THREE: DEATH   31

PART FOUR: THE MAGICIAN   43

PART FIVE: TEMPERANCE   69

PART SIX: THE CHARIOT   79

PART SEVEN: THE WHEEL OF FORTUNE   95

PART EIGHT: THE STAR   107

PART NINE: THE HIEROPHANT   121

ABOUT THE AUTHOR   137

ABOUT CANNABIS NURSING SOLUTIONS   139

SPECIAL THANKS!   143

CONNECT WITH THE AUTHOR   145

Part One

STRENGTH

"Tame your animal instincts and focus on the task at hand."

I s a nurse a survivor or hero? Are they strong or of the most vulnerable? Your answer is determined by what you envision when you think of strength. Do you see a muscular man bench pressing massive weights? Or, a superhero holding together a collapsed bridge, allowing civilians to cross over safely? Most see strength this way, but it is not a physical description. In many cases, strength is depicted as a woman taming a lion without force or coercion, using only subtle, calm, and loving control. Strength is the ability to demonstrate resilience. It is the ability to manage emotions in times of crisis. Strength does not seek to weaken but to encourage the positive expression of passion. Only when true strength is mastered can one truly find the balance to become who they always dreamed of being. We can always find strength among the lessons learned throughout our lifetime.

Nursing is often revered as the most trusted profession, and during the age of COVID-19, nurses were deemed the heroes of the pandemic. Since nurses make up the largest group in hospital staffing, they were right. We were the heroes. We were the heroes surviving through a pandemic. The public saw nurses as heroes, but we saw ourselves as survivors. These differing views beg the question, "Why do those on the outside and those of us within have contrasting ideas about nursing?"

Let's start by discussing how the public sees nurses. The world's view of nurses largely shapes how we see ourselves or, at least, how we want to be perceived. Preconceived notion number one: A nurse must work in a hospital, school, or jail. Preconceived notion number two: The only trajectory that a nurse can see is how to climb the career ladder at that hospital, school, or jail. Based on these preconceived notions, many nurses are not active participants in the healthcare system, even though we are the largest employed staff within the system. We work 12-hour shifts, and somehow, we have glorified working five days a week. For many nurses, the goal is to be an administrator in the hospital. That's the path we believe we must take to achieve that five-day-a-week schedule. My question is: Are you interested in becoming the boss you are being groomed to be?

When we first began our nursing journey, we had a

passion for caring for patients. We are asked the famous question, "Why do you want to be a nurse?" Along the way, the light behind our answer dimmed. Years later, we find ourselves wondering why we started nursing in the first place. Or, worse, we struggle to pinpoint what we are actually passionate about.

We become complacent when we realize we cannot change healthcare or drive decisions. We show up shift after shift, hand out medications, and go home hurt, tired, and drained. We spend our day caring for other people but cannot find the energy to care for ourselves. And even that sacrifice is questionable because are we really caring for patients? We spend most of the day prioritizing and managing our time; therefore, our focus is on our time and the priorities, not the patients.

While we were in nursing school, we learned that there was a specific way to do things, and there was always only one right answer. And since we are constantly considering priorities, we become type A personalities. I mean, how else can we survive high nurse-patient ratios, unmanageable workloads, and trauma-filled days? How many of us look back on when we first saw a patient die in our hands? How many times have you seen somebody take their last breath? How many dead bodies have you washed? How often have you made a mistake, wondered what would happen, but was too scared to tell anyone because you were afraid of losing your license?

You were too busy focused on the priorities to notice your back pain, foot pain, and lack of sleep. When you get home, you are too wired to sleep but in too much pain to move. Maybe you didn't eat dinner when you got home after eight, maybe nine (and that can either be a.m. or p.m.) because your type A personality wouldn't let you leave on time.

How many of us became nurses and chose a specialty we were not passionate about because we were convinced it was the only way to start our nursing career? How many times have we felt stuck because our experience wasn't in the specialty of our choice?

And, let's be honest. When the pandemic hit, did you feel like the hero everyone declared you to be? Did you feel strong? Did you feel like your hospital supported you? Or cared for you? What about PPE? Did you feel protected while you were trying to protect the public? Or, did you feel like a martyr for the cause yet obligated to the profession?

Did fear drive you? Fear of catching covid, fear of not performing to the expectations of the public persona.... Or, was anxiety related to unpredictability the fuel that kept you going? How many times have you questioned your self-worth? How many times did you wonder how long you could continue? How often did you educate your social media about the benefits of vaccinations or even the harms?

If at least one of these questions resonated with you, I am sure you thought about leaving your job and doing something different. But, what do you do when those thoughts arise? When I wrote this book, there were over three million nursing jobs open, which means many of you decided to participate in The Great Resignation. The Great Resignation is what has millions of people in various industries considering quitting their jobs. Some data states that at least 40% of the overall workforce is at least contemplating quitting their jobs.

I spent 13 years working in various jobs before becoming a nurse, but I can truly say that nursing is my passion. I know that I am a nurse for a reason, and I love watching Nurses grow. I understand the nature of our work in most area specialties and the impact it can have on us personally. I am the nurse who started med/surg, although she wanted to be a Pediatric Nurse. I am the nurse who didn't choose the specialty of her choice and felt stuck with nowhere to go and then unhirable. I am the nurse who worked 12-hour shifts and didn't get home until nine after she picked up her baby girl. I am the nurse who was thankful that her aunt fed her baby before I picked her up because I wouldn't have the energy to feed her when I got home. I am the nurse whose body ached from lifting, turning, and washing her patients. I am the nurse who prioritized her patients over her wellbeing.

I was the nurse who searched for something greater than herself but was boxed into her own belief of what a nurse should be. Someone told me I would never work from home because that's not what nurses do. For a while, I believed them.

I am a nurse who loves music and sang to herself to pass the time during long 12-hour shifts. I am also a nurse who identifies herself as an Endocannabinoid Specialty ™ Nurse. Many of us refer to each other as Cannabis Nurses. Cannabis is a new and booming industry, and nurses have a place in this industry. The growth curve for this industry is growing exponentially. There are millions of dollars being made in the legal cannabis market. Cannabis is a win for capitalism, but what about healthcare or for the public at large?

The general population is unaware of what has led to the prohibition. They don't realize that many of the laws regarding cannabis are based on racism and fear. Many of the ideas we have about cannabis are based on prejudices. The media plays a major role in our perception of cannabis. The powers that be don't consider the impact of the War on Drugs and the communities most affected by it. People are rotting away in jail for possessing the same plant people are making millions from today.

There is a multitude of reasons why people love the Cannabis plant. Even though there is a war on drugs and cannabis is illegal, people still choose the plant.

For many people, their love for the plant is based on its ability to save their lives. Although not consciously aware, the general population understands the power the plant can have. Yes, research is limited at this time, mostly because of the schedule I status of cannabis (it sits next to heroin), but there is anecdotal evidence. I hear life-changing stories almost daily about how the plant saved patients' lives. Cannabis can help with nausea and pain and help reduce seizures. Unfortunately, many refuse to see how cannabis can improve the quality of life for a lot of people.

As a nurse, I appreciate a good quality of life. Working the floors and eventually becoming an administrator was the life I lived, but not the life I chose. For years, I didn't know who I was. I could not show gratitude for those who loved me, and I definitely wasn't caring for anyone because I couldn't care for myself. I, too, lacked a quality of life.

It is not my job to fix any of these problems within the system, but it is my job to understand who I am in my role within the system. This book is intended to teach you how to make a change in your career. Each chapter explores my personal experience in the nursing world. Each experience aided in the evolution of my awareness of the intersectionality of Health, Wellness, Nursing, and Black womanhood.

In this book, I will shed some light on what it has taken to enter into an industry not yet inclusive of nurses, let alone our black and brown communities. As we enter a more regulated cannabis space, we are recreating the very systems that put us in a state of prohibition in the first place. The systems that arrest black and brown people at a higher rate are the same systems that allow police brutality and award social inequities.

I chose cannabis nursing as my entrepreneurial goal, but there are no limitations on your choices and where they can take you. The journey to improving your quality of life isn't easy, but it is worth it. And once you realize you were a hero all along, you'll gain the strength you need to be the nurse you knew you should have been all along.

Part Two

THE FOOL

"You are protected even while you're walking off the ledge."

The fool is an interesting archetype. She is naïve and careless due to her ignorance. She is unable to make wise decisions because she has yet to learn the lessons necessary to make them. Think about it. Would you walk off the ledge if you knew what was on the other side? Sometimes, we must discover the other side to learn lessons that will take us on the journey of a lifetime. If you had not walked off the ledge at times in your life, you would be bored and might even return to places you walked away from. So, for me, the only choice is to walk off the ledge. I'll pack a knapsack, put on my headphones, listen to music, and go on the journey with my dog by my side.

Many people associate the fool with something negative. But, in reality, we have all been a fool at some point at the beginning of our journeys. As nurses, we were fools when we decided to take on the profession.

For many of us, nursing school was a time marked by hardship. We spent significant time with our classmates and, at that time, could not have foreseen that we would be friends, colleagues, and bosses together for a lifetime. I learned so much in nursing school, and that expedition became the foundation for everything that would follow. In this part, I will share some of the stories that led me to the profession of nursing and some of my first lessons learned in this journey called life. As you read along, think of the times you were the fool and the lessons you learned as you walked off the ledge to discover the other side.

According to collegefactual.com, approximately 82% of nursing students graduate within six years. This means that almost 20% of students take longer or never graduate from their nursing program. Luckily, I made it in the 82%, but there were moments I was unsure if I would.

The summer after high school graduation, I was an 18-year-old girl trying to figure out where I fit in in life. Graduating from high school was a big deal, and I was proud of my accomplishment. High school graduation marked the completion of a 12-year process that shaped how I saw the world. Also, having my first real boyfriend was the icing on the cake. Who am I kidding? That was the cake. I was dangerously in love...until he broke my heart that summer.

Broken-hearted and determined to prove he lost

a good one, I entered college in the nursing program ready to kick some ass. If there was one thing I was good at, it was school. I loved the academic environment and everything about it: the teachers, the tests, reading. I was there for it all...unless it was hard. I wanted school to be fun all the time.

My decision to attend nursing school was not intentional. I wanted to be a pediatrician or a teacher. I loved children and wanted to stay childlike forever. I was sold the narrative that I would be broke as a teacher, so I chose pediatrics. Becoming a pediatrician sounded hard, so I figured I would break down the steps to pediatrician-ing. First, I would become a nurse, and, in four years, I would be making my own money. Then, I could take care of myself as I went through medical school. That is the way I rationalized it.

Obviously, a pediatrician does not typically take that path. At the time, I had no idea what a nurse was because the two professions are not the same, and being a nurse is not a stepping stone to becoming a pediatrician. Nevertheless, I ignorantly proceeded with my game plan.

My first two semesters in college reminded me of high school, except I sat around between classes. I did not live on campus, so I would sit in lounges and watch The Price Is Right while eating Subway. I took courses like Logic, African American Studies, and

World Literature. World literature (World Lit) was the silliest class on the planet, to me at least. I wanted to be a nurse. How could knowing the world's literature benefit me? World Lit was my first class of the day, and I was always late (a strong indication that I was not feeling it). We were in the colder months, and when I ran across campus to class, my lips would chap. So my late ass was usually applying lip gloss as I walked into World Lit. And every time I did, my teacher would yell at me.

I learned later that my actions were disrespectful based on her cultural norms. In her culture, applying makeup in her presence was offensive. So, in addition to my lateness, I was the absolute worst student she had. I tried my best to be there on time but was unsuccessful. She would put me out of class for my disrespect. I missed a ton of classwork, and I was not engaged in the classes I attended. At the end of it all, I received a D. Yes, it was devastating for a moment, but I eventually figured, "Oh, well. I have to keep going." As far as I was concerned, it wasn't my fault.

Before the next semester, I had to apply to the nursing program and would only be admitted if I passed the Nurse Entrance Test (NET). I believe that is where I met Nadine for the first time, but I was just there to take a test, so meeting her was insignificant to me. I took the test, passed the test, and YAY! I was officially in the nursing program … like, really in the nursing program. After two years of schooling, I could finally take actual nursing classes that I was interested in, like Foundations of Nursing and Anatomy & Physiology.

Semester One in Anatomy & Physiology (A&P) was the first time I realized that school would take effort. That discovery disturbed me; I never had to exert any effort in school. School had always come easy to me. In A&P, I had to memorize organs and parts I did not know existed in the body. That's kind of bizarre, right? Many people live without knowing the way their body works. So, to go into that course and learn about my body without realizing that I was memorizing my body parts was mind-blowing. At the time, I was oblivious and approached A&P as if it were just a class I had to pass. Again, a fool...

That was my second time receiving a failing grade in college, and it wasn't the teacher's fault. My instructor was actually a sweet older man; he just did not take any shit. When you're young and dealing with an adult who doesn't let anything slide, you get annoyed. I did not like him because I thought he was supposed to ensure I passed the tests. Unfortunately, just like my World Lit professor, my A&P instructor had discretion on how he ran his classroom. He spoke low and fast and expected us to care enough to hear what he said.

My instructor threw tons of information at us in every class I attended. We discussed the musculoskeletal unit and learned about bones, cartilage, ligaments, tendons, and connective tissues. We learned about all 206 bones and how they support our body, store calcium, and support our red blood cells. We learned about hyaline, fibrous, and elastic cartilage. I remember looking at them through a microscope. That was pretty cool. We learned about the joints, movable joints, immovable joints, the 600 muscles, a majority of the 900 ligaments, and a bunch of the 4000 tendons. I was overwhelmed, and as I said, my instructor didn't take any shit. He believed we could learn the information if we gave our best effort.

Either he was wrong, or we didn't try hard enough. When we tested on the muscles, the whole class failed. To me, that indicated I had not done anything wrong. If everyone else failed, it was okay that I failed. He graded the muscles exam on a curve. Instructors typically grade on a curve when they don't want to seem like the bad guy. The highest grade in the class becomes the true north, and, in that class, the true north was a girl named Deena.

I spoke with Deena occasionally. She was concerned about keeping up with the coursework while being pregnant. I thought it was interesting that she was pregnant while learning about bones, muscles, and tendons. I was overwhelmed, but I knew she was even more overwhelmed. Even with the curve, I got a failing mark on the test. How could I fail a test I really" tried" to pass? How could anyone pass a test like that? It's too many muscles, ligaments, and tendons for anyone to remember. How could anyone be expected to remember all that stuff? Learning the material was unrealistic, and I did not perform well. I limited my abilities. After staring at my failing score for a few minutes, I stood and walked to the bathroom.

I could not hold back the tears. As soon as I walked through the bathroom door, I broke down. The only person I could think to call was my mom; I knew she could help me. An emotional wreck, I spewed out all the reasons I shouldn't have failed before she could even answer the phone. I went on and on about how unfair my professor was, how complicated the test was, blah blah blah. Much like my professor, my mom didn't take any shit either. After hearing as much of my whining as she could take, she said, "I did not choose this. You did. So figure it out." Her short and harsh reply cut through me for a couple of reasons. Number one: She was right. You fool, why didn't you think about that before? This is something you want to accomplish! Why weren't you trying? Where is your confidence, young lady? Anybody can memorize anything! Number two: Why can't she protect me from this? I felt a little betrayed. I felt like I deserved to be protected. At that moment, I knew I had to protect myself. But, how? My only solution was to do something different. So, I did.

I started studying, like really studying. However, I lacked the skills to do it properly. I realized that straining does not indicate doing. Intention only gets you as far as the intent; doing takes you where you need to go. Nobody ever taught me to study, so it was trial and error. I tried note-taking techniques, mnemonics, highlighters, and everything I could think of. In the end, I got a C. Luckily for me, the grades were graded on a curve.

Next up, Foundations of Nursing. That was it: The Real Deal! We learned about miter corners, bed baths, turning, and positioning. It was exciting, but for some reason, I still performed at a mediocre level, according to my teachers. One day, we received the results of a test, and I got a C. I had studied my ass off but made a C. How could that be? I obviously did not do something right, and I had to protect myself. I started to observe my environment. While I sulked about my C, I overheard the teacher tell another young lady, "Good job!"

What? Had she gotten all the questions right? I turned to discover it was Deena, the young lady from A&P who was concerned about her pregnancy. I learned that she had a little girl and later had the pleasure of watching her grow up. I realized that I needed to be friends with Deena and learn how she did it because I needed help. Failure was not an option.

I often started to see Nadine (the girl I met while

taking the NET). We took Microbiology the same semester. Weirdly enough, she always told me about her personal life. It seemed out of nowhere too. I thought it was strange that she was so open about her life. I am generally a reserved person who doesn't share unless I am comfortable. Well, I guess Nadine was comfortable with me. She told me about her baby daddy, some abusive situations, money issues, and everything in between. I shouldn't have been taken aback by her openness. Often, people randomly shared their personal details with me. I didn't mind it most times. It was usually someone who needed help and found comfort in sharing their struggles with me. However, at times, I confused the comfort with friendship.

I realized that Nadine was friends with Deena, so I decided to engage. I wanted Nadine to get to know me, and I hoped we could be friends. In my head, it was possible because she was so comfortable sharing her life with me. We became great friends, and this was when my experience in nursing school changed. It was not because I manipulated a situation and immediately got excellent grades; I did not. I passed nursing school with a 2.8 GPA. Okay, more like a 2.78. Anyway, my experience shifted because I was happy I found a group of girls I could connect with.

Nadine, Deena, and later, Crystal and a white lady named Riley became my study and friend group. We met often. We would study all day, quiz each other, and when we were done, we would party and party hard. We were so pressed to go to Love the Club in DC. We would fill our water bottles with water during the day and liquor at night. Going to an inner-city school, you tend to hang out with friends from the inner city and adopt their lifestyle as your own. I loved it.

Undergrad was a fantastic experience because I was exposed to the world in a way I had been largely sheltered from. I also was accepted in a way that did not require me to be perfect. I just had to show up and be me. There were good times and bad times, good teachers and bad ones.

My favorite teacher wore a wig that looked like a bird's nest. I figured she couldn't afford a good wig. She never knew what she was talking about but leaned on the fact that she had authority, and we would still listen. And, there was that time I got a whopping 28% on a written assignment. That means I nearly failed the entire assignment. Who can get an entire assignment wrong?! I did.

My first clinical placement gave me a rude awakening about the world of nursing. Clinicals were experiences in various healthcare settings curated by the instructor. My first clinical was in a nursing home. I arrived at my clinical placement in a lighthearted manner. We had to get there at seven AM, and that was early. Who gets up that early? For the first few weeks, we worked on interpersonal communication, which sounded silly at the time. Looking back, I realize it is an essential skill many people lack. We had to review a patient's chart and determine what our assessment questions would be. I wrote mine out very quickly and told my instructor, "I am done." She instructed me to practice on a patient. She wanted me to take that patient's chart, figure out where the patient was, and initiate a professional relationship with the patient. I was glad she sent me with a partner, but my partner and I were equally as nervous.

We bickered back-and-forth for a bit, figuring out what to do and how to do it. The funny thing is, all we had to do was look at the chart for the room number, walk into the room, and talk to the patient. Eventually, we got there. We walked into the room, and the patient was lying on a pink blowup bed. There was some sort of machine connected to the blowup bed, and it was loud. I later learned the contraption was a way to relieve pressure on the skin to support the healing of pressure ulcers or prevent ulcers from forming in high-risk patients. Oh, yeah, and the patient that was lying there was butt-naked.

That was the first time I had seen a naked patient. We walked in and walked right back out, thinking there had to have been an error. Why would I talk to a patient while they were naked? Somebody should have warned me. The patient did not look like he was ready to talk. I did not know that nurses talked to naked patients. As I said, I chose the nursing path, thinking it would take me to medical school. There I was, about a year and a half before graduation, still clueless about a nurse's job.

Even after that, I kept going through nursing school because I had made it pretty far. I planned to graduate in 2007, but I graduated in 2008. I was foolishly devastated by the delay. While preparing for my senior year, I learned there was a required class I had not taken. The class wouldn't be available until the following year. It was also a prerequisite for everything to come, so I couldn't move forward to other classes without it. It was hard to believe my advisor would not advise me about the order of my classes and how they impacted my graduation. I could only take one class the next semester, so I worked at the bank that year.

Working as a teller, a former LPN told me that I would not make it as a nurse. That was a challenging year because I was not moving toward my goals. The world had to have been playing a trick on me. My life was on pause. I couldn't move out of my place when I planned. I threw many tantrums because life wasn't fair. That was another time I allowed my emotions to take over something I knew I could not control. Nevertheless, I trudged through that year, finding joy in music and friends. I took an extra class called Sociolinguistics, and it happened to be one of my favorite classes. I learned that anything outside of my control was intended to teach me the necessary lessons.

World lit eventually came back to haunt me, but luckily, based on a technicality, I was still able to graduate in 2008. I graduated with my girls, and I was so proud! In general, undergrad had been difficult for me. It was the first time I realized that life was not easy. I could not easily pass the tests; I had to truly study. The instructors were strict, and it wasn't over yet. I still had to take the NCLEX. We were all terrified of the NCLEX because if we did not pass that test, all our time in school would have been pointless. I barely passed the exit exam, so my anxiety was high. I passed the NCLEX on my first try, but only by the skin on my teeth (I got all the questions it can give). Finally, it was time to begin my journey as a nurse. The summer after graduation was the last time my study group would be a group. We no longer needed each other, so we disbanded for various reasons. So there I was, out in the world alone. I was a nurse but alone and still a fool with many more lessons to learn.

Part Three

DEATH

"Transformation is never easy; you must kill off who you once were in order to become who you are supposed to be."

D eath is largely misunderstood. When someone dies, we are typically saddened and mourn the moments we spent with them in their physical state. Through our tears, we cleanse and restore balance in our bodies, similar to how the rain washes the earth.

As a nurse, I've seen more death than the average person. So naturally, the way I see death has been shaped largely by that experience. I've grown to see death as a beautiful gift. It is a transition to a different phase of existence. Rather than be saddened about each dying patient, I deem it an honor to be in the presence of a human during the last days of their current existence and watch them journey into their next. Death, in a metaphorical sense, is very similar. There are moments in our lives when we are forced to leave the person we want to be and become the person we are required to be. Though it marks the emergence of new life, I believe pregnancy is also a metaphorical death. During those nine months, mothers prepare physically and mentally for their new existence as a mother. The woman that once existed can no longer live — she must become a mom. Or, at least that's what I thought.

I had been a nurse for two years. For the first three months, I was in orientation. For the following three months, I had a mentor. After that, I was off to the races. At that time, I was still very young, and my body could tolerate the 12-hour shifts and strenuous labor. Since I only worked three days a week, I had four days to have a good time! As far as I was concerned, things were going pretty well. I was positive I was getting the hang of being a nurse. I had adapted to some of the crazy sightings in my unit and grown accustomed to waking up before the sun rose and returning home well after sunset. Then, I was asked to be a charge nurse.

What? Why? How are we calling me a charge nurse? I definitely did not have the skills. I did not see myself as a leader. If that wasn't enough, they also wanted me to be a preceptor. Everything sounded crazy. I felt as if I was being thrown to the wolves. My job was calling me a leader, and I couldn't see what they saw in me. Either way, I went with the flow...until I found out I was pregnant.

Working as a pregnant nurse on the floors was a feat. That was my first indication that long hours on my feet would not be a long-term solution for my career. The extra weight in my abdomen and the swelling that would occur from being on my feet all day caused me to break down at the end of the day. Let's not mention the nausea. I had a patient during a rapid response who needed suctioning, and the gurgling would make me sick to my stomach. I remember the rapid response turning into a code, and as they were calling the code, I was running out of the room to vomit. As I jetted to the nearest restroom, my team asked, "Where is the nurse?"

By the time I finished vomiting, my patient was being transferred. They ensured I suffered the consequences; the bed was left in the ICU, and I had a new patient ready to fill it immediately. My unit was on the sixth floor, and the ICU was on the second floor, so I had to take the elevator down, find a bed, roll it to the elevator, and ride back up. Sounds pretty easy, but not for a woman, seven months pregnant, trying to steer and navigate the bed alone. It's difficult for two people to steer and navigate those wide beds.

Near the end of my pregnancy, I asked my manager if there was any other work I could do. I often heard the term 'light duty' thrown around but apparently, there was no light duty for me. My manager told me, "We have all been pregnant working these floors, and you will be no different." I had two choices: take my FMLA at eight months pregnant or get back to my patients. This was my second indication that nursing could not be my long-term career solution. I could not believe the disregard for the baby growing in my belly. No one seemed to care that I needed a way to care for myself and my baby while making a living. I continued working until it was time for me to give birth.

My daughter was born at 7lbs 7oz. When I looked into her eyes for the first time, she had the most entrancing gaze. I saw the purest form of love deep in the universe of her eyes. I saw the source, and it spoke to me in an indescribable way. The only thing I could verbalize is that her name is Madisyn. My husband and I had already named her, but I wasn't sure until that moment. She looked at me as though she had always known who I was. I knew she existed for me as I for her.

The day Madisyn was born was the most amazing day of my life. I realized that I had never loved anyone more than I loved her. My world shifted gently yet forcefully. I could feel it. At the time, I thought the shift was hormones. The love I had for Madisyn was so overwhelming I could have exploded. I did not know where to put it all. I officially added a new layer to my identity. "I am a mother. Woooooooow." I said to myself. I was a daughter, a sister, a nurse, a wife, and now, a mother. I was excited to try this cool thing called mom-ing. I believe most moms envision what their lives will be like after the birth of their first child. I did. I imagined a warm and cozy home. My mom and sister would cook dinner for me, hang out around the house, wash clothes, hold the baby, and offer nurturing advice. I imagined my best friends (the ones I partied with in undergrad) hanging out with Madisyn and me, chatting and drinking wine, giggling about silly things, and watching Girlfriends all day. I imagined having the support of a beautiful network of people. Unfortunately, life after birthing my daughter was nothing like I imagined.

My husband worked from 3 PM to 11 PM. He had been working that shift since I'd known him, but it didn't impact me until Madisyn was born. I barely saw him, and he was always asleep when she was awake. He didn't get home until midnight and went to bed around 2 or 3 AM, which meant he slept late in the morning. And, as many of you probably know, infants wake up every two to three hours. My husband was generally kind, gentle, and very supportive, but waking every two to three hours strains a brand-new mother. I struggled with breastfeeding, and I was in so much pain from the C-section I could not walk up and down the steps. I was not allowed to drive, so I was stuck in a small apartment all day, waiting for my husband to return from work. The shift he worked served us because we would only need a sitter for four to five hours when I had to go back to work. We did not want to change our lives any more than they already had. The best part of it all was that I had Madisyn. She was so important to me, but looking back, I treated her more like a doll than an actual human. It felt as if she tied me down and sucked away the life I once had. It was such a confusing feeling. How could I love someone so much but feel so alone and unprotected?

My emotions were haywire. I cried about the pain of my c section scar. I cried about having to make myself dinner. I cried about being alone. I cried about a Facebook post. Everything made me cry. It was a challenging time for me. One day, I broke down and called a close relative. They offered some straightforward advice I disagreed with, and their response was, "You will not make a good mother because you don't listen."

I believed them and committed to proving them wrong, but being a good mother goes beyond saying, "I'll be a good mother." Nevertheless, I was on a mission and set the most unattainable standards for myself. Of course, this created even more pressure for me. I eventually realized that mothering was not what I imagined it would be.

Oh, and my friends? Well, their lives continued without me. They went to parties, hung out with new friends, met guys, flew to Miami, and snapped pics for Facebook. One evening, I invited some friends over for dinner. My husband loves to cook, and he's really good at it. He worked the midday shift, so he had no regard for everyone else's eating patterns. He wouldn't cook until 1 or 2 AM, and the crazy thing was, they would wait. On that particular night, we were having a good time when one of my friends told me that she loved her dog almost as much as I love my daughter.

I could not process my daughter being compared to a dog. I know people love their dogs, but I pushed Madisyn out of my womb. "What?" I responded. "How can you love your dog as much as I love this human that was cut from my body? What?" That did not make any sense to me. The rest of that conversation did not go very well, and the party was over.

Then, there were the in-laws. My in-laws did not accept me as a part of their family for years. They felt as if I intruded on their family dynamic and stole the baby (my husband) from the family. Once, my husband and I allowed an in-law to keep Madisyn overnight. We would see them at a baby shower we were all invited to the following day. We were so thankful they kept our daughter, but I was excited to see my baby girl the next day. It was hard to imagine any amount of time away from her. It's a catch 22 of sorts. I needed time to sleep, relax, and recoup, but I never wanted her to leave my side. When Madisyn was gone, I felt like a part of me was missing.

When we arrived at the baby shower, Madisyn and

the in-laws were already there. Of course, I couldn't wait to hold my baby. My parents always taught me to be polite, especially among people I do not know well. However, I noticed my in-laws were trying to give my almost 1-year-old Hawaiian Punch! I was not okay with that. I informed them that I did not want Madisyn to have Hawaiian Punch, but they did not take my response well. "What is your problem? Madisyn has been drinking juice all night long," my in-law replied.

As I would have responded to anyone caring for my child, I told them I would appreciate it if they didn't give Madisyn sugary juice; she was too young. Their spouse leaned over to me and said something under their breath. I responded, "What did you say?" The next thing I know, my in-law is standing over me, calling me all types of bitches and hoes, pointing their finger in my face as if we were at the club and she had just caught me twerking on her man.

I was shocked. An older adult had never treated me that way. I always tried to be respectful, but her actions warranted a different response. My husband came out of nowhere, stood up for me, and cursed her out. That was a sight I'd never seen before in my life.

At that moment, I knew my in-lawe did not fuck with me. Unfortunately, that was the nature of our relationship for years to come. Yet another relationship that did not flourish as I imagined. Once again, I felt alone. Although my husband had stood up for me, he ultimately accepted the behavior, and I did not feel safe or protected. My life had become so different. Everything around me was negative, except Madisyn. The only light I saw was in my daughter's eyes, but she could not talk, so I still felt alone. The person I once was had died. She died the moment I gave birth to my daughter. The relationships I had before Madisyn either changed or disappeared. When I went to work, I was so overwhelmed with everything happening around me I would cry.

Calling the residents, especially third or fourth-year residents, was stressful. Sometimes, they would yell at us when we did not have a full assessment. I typically brushed it off, but now, it stung differently. I cried at least once every shift during that time. One day, someone caught me crying and suggested I go to a therapist. I brushed it off until I realized I didn't know how to proceed independently. I did not know what was going to happen next in my life. I couldn't see beyond the clouds of chaos hovering around me.

So, I began my quest for a therapist. How do you find a therapist? Well, first, you find out who accepts your insurance. Contrary to what you may believe, hospital benefits are not that great. It was hard to find a therapist who would take my insurance. As a black woman, my preference is a black therapist, but they are few and far between. The next step was to find a therapist with credentials that supported what I needed, hopefully within 15 minutes away. There were none.

I had to drive 45 minutes to get to my therapist twice a week. I also went to my OB/GYN for check-ups, but she was so busy our appointments were 10 minutes or maybe even less. One day during a check-up, I told her about my mental state, and she immediately wrote me a prescription for an antidepressant. An antidepressant and therapy? Perfect. It seemed like I had a solution for my problem. I committed to both and hoped for the best.

When I started therapy, the focus seemed to be my relationship with my family. It annoyed me that she wanted to talk about my family. There were many other situations I wanted to discuss, but we never really got to it. The driving distance and lack of clarity on the goals and outcomes of our relationship were disheartening. So, I stopped going.

I took the pills prescribed by my OBGYN for a few weeks, and things did not improve. On the contrary, everything seemed to get worse. I was sadder than ever. I would hold my daughter while she was supposed to be on tummy time and cry in the dark for what seemed like hours at a time. Since they weren't working, I stopped taking the antidepressants.

One day, I woke up with the urge to get a master's degree in nursing education. I did not question it. I do not know what provoked the thought, but as I was precepting weeks prior, I felt more alive and happy than I had in a while.

I thought back to the summer after high school when I decided to be a nurse though I also wanted to be a teacher. "Why can't I have the best of both worlds?" I asked myself. I could be a teacher and a nurse. That evening, I stayed up late, excited for my husband to come home from work so I could share my revelation. He was exhausted that night. After I shared the news, he responded, "Where did this come from?" He didn't realize it then, but we would have conversations like this repeatedly. I explained my need to focus on something outside of the house, grow beyond the hospital job that made me miserable, and be more than a mother. He understood and supported my new path forward.

After the conversation with my husband, I focused on getting a new start and applied for a master's degree in nursing education. That was a brand-new start, and as I completed the application for my program, I realized that I could pull myself out of anything.

When I first became a mother, I wanted to throw myself into motherhood. I lost sight of myself and my identity. The world was happening to me. I lost control of my moods, environment, social network, and self. There was no way I could be a good mother and not demonstrate a strong identity for myself. The darkest moments are usually an indication that I need to do something different. Ashley died and was reborn. She needed to experience the transition into a new version of herself. Though I didn't know it at the time, that wouldn't be my last transition.

Part Four

THE MAGICIAN

"Your potential has no limits; give your body permission be the conduit for the magic you are destined to create."

W hat comes to mind when you think of a magician? Do you imagine a guy wearing a black top hat, putting on a performance with a rabbit or some other unfortunate creature? Do you imagine a man waving a stick and making a woman dressed like Vanna White disappear, then reappear? Since childhood, that is how many have been programmed to perceive magic. We don't realize how this perception causes us to function in a self-limiting belief system. This ingrained belief system about magicians removes the possibility of you being able to produce your own magic. Magic is simply creating the energy to attract like energy, thus perpetuating a change. It is up to you and your subconscious to generate the energy necessary to evoke change in your life. Think about the magical things that have happened in your lifetime. How often did you do it on purpose? How often have you said, "I can't believe that happened to me?" Now, consider how it was attracted to you.

As children, we are told what to do, how to think, how to behave based on societal norms. Going through nursing school or any other educational system reinforces this way of being. Our educational systems were built as tools to teach us to function based on one perspective. However, there are millions of perspectives and billions of ways to accomplish one thing.

It's easy to live our lives as if the world is happening to us and we can't make our own decisions. But, at some point, we must evolve and determine to take charge of our lives. Every decision we make leads us to the next decision. The decisions can be simple things like the food we choose to eat, the stands we take, our friend selections, and the career we decide to pursue.

After letting the world happen to me for far too long, I decided to make a change. Making that decision was the magic I needed, and it led me to a series of events that I could not have foreseen. But, similar to the fool, I'd rather experience the bumps and bruises (aka jump off the ledge) than stay where I was. Now I know every obstacle was purposed to make me stronger.

According to nurse.com, in 2018, only 4% of nurses worked per diem, and 46% of nurses planned to leave their jobs. This was before COVID-19. Nurses generally tend to job hop. It is common for nurses to hold more than one job in the healthcare arena, but it is less common for nurses to travel and work per diem. I decided to work in three float pools as per diem staff. I chose to do what many of my counterparts were not doing.

While I worked in multiple float pools, I worked on obtaining my master's degree. That decision gave me the flexibility to control my work assignments. I worked when I needed to make a certain amount of money, and there was no penalty if I decided to complete an assignment for school instead of working. Plus, I got paid more per hour. I could work fewer hours, make more money, go to school, and take care of Madisyn. Around that time, Madisyn was a toddler.

I loved working in the float pools, and I got mad love on the units. People looked to me as the expert, and I felt like a hero, saving the short-staffed units. When I arrived, they were appreciative. They would show their appreciation through the assignments they gave me or by inviting me to the unit potlucks. I loved being a part of each unit's culture, learning how the collective units functioned and understanding what charged them emotionally.

Each unit has its energetic aura, and as a floater, I had to assess the tone of every atmosphere. Some hospitals have consistent energy from unit to unit, and those hospitals were generally stale and boring.

You knew what to expect on every unit, and they flowed the same everywhere you went. From a process improvement standpoint, that is ideal for better patient outcomes. From a humanistic standpoint, it was just boring.

In other hospitals, the energy varies. Hospitals can be functional and dysfunctional at the same time. It can be slightly chaotic on one unit and smooth-sailing on another unit. The love can be palpable on one unit and the drama equally noticeable on another. Since the time I spent on the different units wasn't extensive, the events that happened on my shift could not alter my emotional state. I knew there was an end, and I was genuinely happy to be there.

As a floater, aids or techs may not support you because there is a lack of understanding between the two roles. Sometimes, the responsibilities of the nurse and the aid overlap. It is the nurse's job to delegate to the aid, but, at the same time, the aid generally has responsibilities that are specific to a unit and the patients' needs. The aid could choose whether or not to complete certain tasks, but ultimately, the nurse's license is at risk. The nurse must ensure tasks are completed in a timely fashion. Techs know this and often take advantage of nurses, especially if they feel like they are being taken advantage of. The presence of this behavior depends on the unit's culture and the nurse's ability to communicate. It begs the question:

Are nurses really heroes? It seems as if the aids have all the power.

The techs never treated me poorly, probably because I did not mind turning, cleaning, or straight catheterizing a patient. They respected my willingness to do the "dirty "work. Some nurses feel that part of the job is beneath them and when techs feel (or assume) the condescension, they rebel. They will leave the nurse high and dry or refuse to do certain things. I know this because I worked as a tech during my nursing school days, and those were issues we complained about.

Anyway, working as a floater was a great time in my life. I was achieving something and was very excited about the many opportunities before me. I felt freer and more appreciated. Life was good.

After 2.5 years of working in the float pools and going to school, I finally received my degree. I was comfortable working in the float pools, so I continued working as if I was not a master's prepared nurse. Six months after graduation, I met up with Deena for drinks. We got drunk, shared our career goals, and complained about life. The next day, she offered me a position in a Transition to Practice Program she was building as the Nurse Residency Program manager at a hospital over 1.5 hours away. Deena believed the facilitator position would be a good fit for me based on where I wanted my career to go. That was too good to be true and came from nowhere, but she was right.

The magic was happening.

Initially, I was told it was a flexible position, which was important to me since I was transitioning from complete autonomy as a floater to being confined by the requirements of a job. Then, the position changed from a 40-hour position to a salaried position because the sister hospital had recorded my position as a salaried position. I didn't appreciate that. I thought I could work four ten-hour days or three 12-hour days and a four-hour shift to make my 40 hours and get overtime pay as an hourly employee. I was used to hustling my hours, and I wanted to keep it that way. As much as I wanted things to remain the same, I prioritized progressing my career and helping new grads. So, I settled for the adjustment.

The Transition to Practice Program was my first five days a week job. I had only dreamed of working five days a week. When I worked in the float pool, I loved when I would head out at three PM, but that was in relation to getting off at seven and with no consideration of doing it every day. I was excited that the sun was still up when I left work. It was the consistency I had always desired. I knew how I would spend my day and when I would eat lunch or dinner.

The way the hospital functioned was a culture shock for me. I was most familiar with horizontal dynamics, but that was my first time exposed to vertical dynamics. In this new role, I learned about the hospital as a system. The culture shock of how hospital organizations operate was eye-opening. I was frequently confused about the nice nasty emails, underhanded comments in meetings, and dynamics between people competing for certain positions of power. It was crazy, and I figured it was because I had been so disconnected as a float pool nurse. That's it. I had to have been the problem, and I needed to adjust. I'll let you be the judge. Let me tell you about two situations that greatly awakened me to hospital culture's effect on people.

First, let's discuss one of the grads I worked with named Lisa. Lisa wanted to be a cardiovascular intensive care unit (CVICU) nurse. In nursing school, she worked on a medical-surgical (med-surg) unit as a tech. Lisa was quiet, but I could tell she came from an environment that caused her to distrust people. She had a daughter and was a single mom, which let me know she was responsible or at least would get shit done. She was brown but did not have all-black features. She had a slight accent that gave me the hint of Latina vibes, and she was so sweet. The Transition to Practice Program was designed to expose new grads to different units in the hospital. The new grad would experience units based on the specialty they were hired for. My job was to ensure they got the experience intended and felt supported. Lisa was in a cohort of five, so I had plenty of time to get to know them all. She struggled, not because she could not do the work, but the preceptors left her high and dry. If you are a quiet, introverted nurse and refuse to ask for what you want, you won't get what you need.

New grads spent a week in some units or two months in other units. They were in new environments with new people frequently. This experience was not good for Lisa's personality type. She needed to spend more time with people to trust them and be open to gaining their trust. When I asked Lisa questions about how and why she hung iv's, she always answered appropriately. If I challenged her on her prioritization, she always had solid rationales. Though she did well, the staff reported that Lisa was not performing. It was strange. What I saw and what they said did not match up.

Gossip spreads fast in a hospital. So when Lisa finally arrived at her home unit, she already had a reputation. The clinical leader, Susan, had her eye on Lisa from the jump. Susan had been a CVICU nurse for 500 years. She knew everything there was to know about nursing in an ICU. She was a wealth of knowledge but closed-minded to new ideas. She only listened to you if you were connected to leadership. It was very difficult dealing with Susan. She expected the nurses to hear her lecture on extracorporeal membrane oxygenation (ECMO) once and have it all together. She could not understand why different teaching methods were important or why certain concepts needed to be retaught.

So, Lisa had a reputation, and Susan had already judged her. Lisa made a few mistakes, and her whole ICU career was questioned. It was a challenge to work in that ICU. The nurses experienced at least one death a day and sometimes treated three patients at a time, which meant there was potential for all three patients to die. The culture was dog-eat-dog, predominately white, and the few nurses of color on the unit had proven their ability. Unfortunately, Lisa did not come in ready to eat with the wolves. She wanted to help patients and knew that if her cohorts pulled out the side of her that they wanted, she would be uncontrollable. At least, that is what I perceived.

Susan wanted Lisa out. Others would say things like, "She just doesn't cut it. She cannot perform," but I fought for Lisa and pushed back. It was exhausting because I had to fight against intangibles, not facts. Every day Lisa worked, I had to be in her unit to observe her work and the preceptors who taught her. Susan, Lisa, and I met weekly to discuss Lisa's progress and develop detailed goals. Every resident meeting included a conversation about Lisa. Eventually, leadership caved, Lisa achieved every goal and was allowed to stay. To my knowledge, Lisa worked in that ICU for at least three years.

Then, there was Georgia. Georgia was a dark,

brown-skinned, petite young lady. She wore her hair in weaves and had a gentle voice. She knew what she wanted and was driven. Georgia knew that The Transition to Practice Program was not the end of her story. She told me she was going to be a nurse anesthetist.

Georgia's situation was very similar to Lisa's, but I refused to be backed into a wall this time around. Fighting for Lisa was worth it, and I knew I had the power to do it, but it was emotionally taxing. By the time I got to Georgia, I had worked in the program for over a year. I never acclimated to the work environment and strived daily to preserve my energy. When the situation with Georgia arose, I was exhausted and lacked the evidence to support my position. In addition, Georgia came in with a cohort of 13, so I did not spend as much time with her as I had with Lisa.

After a year in the game, I was aware of the culture I was dealing with, so I backed down. They dismissed Georgia, and I felt guilty because I knew she was capable. Truthfully, anyone can be a nurse on any unit. The tasks are repetitive, especially on specialized units, because the patient scenario is always the same. Sometimes, it takes people a little longer to pick up on the patterns. And, as I stated earlier, closed mouths did not get fed.

Anywho, Georgia and I were both devastated. Though I was in self-preservation mode and felt drained, I couldn't shake the feelings of guilt. How could I have let that happen to a good person, knowing the impact it could have on her? However, Georgia was determined. Eventually, she became a Nurse Anesthetist, just like she said she would. That's what I call creating your own magic.

Speaking of magic, let's get back to the experience that taught me to create my own. So, I was considered hospital leadership and co-created and facilitated programming with no formal training. It was an exciting time, the best job I ever held, and the most fulfilling so far, but there was a 1.5-hour commute. Over time, I began to feel disempowered. Additionally, my husband hurt his back at work. Working at that job, I could potentially become the program manager or even climb the career ladder and become a director.

One day, I received a job solicitation email from a hospital closer to home that had a similar program. Since my husband had hurt his back, home life and my ability to manage my life became more challenging. So, I decided to pursue the job that seemed to have fallen in my lap. Taking that job seemed to be the easiest solution to all my troubles.

That position paid less, but since it was closer to home, I figured it balanced out financially: less commute, less gas, and less time. In the interview with the manager, I explained my vision for the position. I spoke about preceptor workshops, developing new nurses, and providing support for the nurses on the unit, such as access to educational resources. I felt it was a good interview, but I was probably blinded by my need to make a change. I was eventually offered the position, but for some reason, I was not excited about taking it. Life has taught me that your intuition is never wrong.

The hardest part was telling Deena I would be quitting her program. I had quit jobs before, but that time it hurt. It felt like I was letting a lot of people down. One day, while making my rounds on the OB nurses, I stopped by their directors' office to talk about one nurse but ended up talking about myself. I felt like I needed to defend my decision, share who I felt I was letting down, and everything in between. Deena listened, and her response was simply, "Forgive yourself."

I had never heard that before, and I didn't think I deserved to forgive myself. To be honest, I struggled to prioritize myself. I rarely thought about my needs. I was too busy chasing what I thought I needed to accomplish. I wanted the five-day work schedule, and I got that. I liked the idea of being hospital leadership and the power I had, but those conditions were egotistical reasons why I needed to stay. That particular transition was challenging because it forced me to fight my ego. Confronting the ego is necessary to unblock the magic we deserve but don't think the ego won't fight until its death. Your ego does not want you to experience inspired action. It prefers to distort reality and manipulate conditions to appear as what you need.

My last workday was on a Friday, and I started at my new job the next Monday. Working at the new hospital was a very disorienting experience, but leaving one environment on a Friday and arriving in a completely different environment on a Monday was especially unsettling. It was like being lost in a whirlwind, then being picked up by a different whirlwind. I was comfortable in the first whirlwind. I knew what cows I would run into, the furniture that would hit me, and I could see my path forward. That Monday brought on new cows, new furniture, and a totally different vision. I was not okay, but I tried to make the most of it.

Nursing orientation in every hospital is always daunting. You spend a week with PowerPoints and some depressed instructor who hates their job, mumbling about the same information taught in nursing school. You demonstrate blood draws on a dummy that already has holes in it. You put Foley catheters in dummies that don't have the actual anatomy of a human. And sometimes, when the instructors really want to get interactive, they'll have you do your fingerstick to ensure they properly put your information into the system. Finally, you get your badge, you are told hospital policies, and you walk away, expected to perform at optimal levels.

After orientation, I went to my assigned unit, and that's when I met Karmen. Karmen was a fairly young Filipino lady. She worked on the unit for over ten years, knew everybody in the hospital, and had all the policies memorized. Moments after we met, she began rambling about all the policies. As I listened, I wondered why she gave me so much clinical information, but I figured I had to have a solid foundation, so I needed to be aware. Then, I was instructed to shadow a nurse on the unit, which was confusing because my job was to create a professional development program. I realized they actually needed clinical direction and clinical support.

During my interview, I made it clear that the intermediate care unit (IMCU) was above my personal experience of acuity; my background was med-surg and telemetry, not IMCU. When I expressed my concerns, I received quite a bit of pushback. I was told that was what I signed up for, and the staff on the unit questioned my experience. There was no appreciation for the professional development specialty on that unit.

The nurses on IMCU were overworked and burned out. The patient ratios were supposed to be four-to-one, but they would get ICU-level patients. ICU nurses generally get a two-to-one ratio. Morally, I didn't agree with some decisions made for new nurses or any nurses, for that matter.

I worked the night shift, thinking it would be a good fit for me, but it was not. My second infant was at home during the day when I was supposed to be sleeping. I was allowed to work based on the schedules of the new graduates. One night, I came into work with Tasha, and she was crying, yelling, and fussing about a patient who arrived at the IMCU from the emergency department (ED) with a thready pulse, and the patient needed to be vented. IMCU did not have vents, but since ICU was full at that time, the supervisors sent the patient to our unit instead. He should have stayed in the ED so they could monitor his status.

The patient could have potentially been on his last breath, but we knew we could not help him. I don't remember all the details, but the patient was eventually transferred to another unit. As if that weren't bad enough, the staff began to gossip about Tasha and I being 'subpar nurses' because we did not keep him on the unit. They thought we should have kept him despite our assessments that he did not belong there. They whispered about how they would have helped him and what they would have done. However, none offered to help when the patient was on the IMCU floor.

That kind of gossip became the norm. I was judged often and constantly needed to prove myself to the rest of the staff on the unit. Karmen was clinically strong and also THE Gossip Queen. She frequently asked me to do clinical work on behalf of the staff. I was expected to enter patient rooms that were not mine and relieve the staff; I did, for the most part.

One day, I went to draw the blood of a patient who happened to be an IV drug user. He guided me to which vein to use. He said, "Girl, I have a Cadillac of veins." I thought he was funny, and though he was joking, it was true. He was such an easy stick.

After a long night on my feet, my manager requested to meet with me. She informed me that we were getting a new nurse to the unit. Her name was Yiva, and she was from a unit across the hall. Apparently, she did not get along with any of the staff, but they didn't want to fire her. Management thought she would thrive on a higher acuity unit and expected me to keep a close eye on her.

Yiva was a black American who wore perfect weaves, had perfectly chocolate skin, and had tons of confidence. At first glance, I could tell she'd had a hard life, but I could not determine if it were because she had just gotten out of a challenging situation or if she had a complex background. Yiva had a terrible attitude and didn't get along with anyone. I heard whispers of her cursing out nurses just about every night she worked. Assuming I was in a position of authority, Yiva attempted to get along with me. She soon realized I had no real authority and revealed her true colors. Yiva lied often. She would say she distributed medicine but didn't. She could not calculate drugs and lied about that too.

My experience with her was mind-boggling. Work became tumultuous the moment she arrived at our unit. I could see that she was not performing, was disruptive to the unit, and was clinically incapable of caring for patients. In the beginning, I thought she had an issue with time management and tried to assist her until I caught her on the computer, scrolling the Internet. When I tried to explain her behavior, no one believed me. I was told that I could not determine her clinical competency because I wasn't clinically competent. Yiva was eventually fired because she was accused of hitting a patient, and I was mind-blown. It felt as if I were in an alternate reality. I recalled how at my previous job, Georgia performed well but was still fired. At the new job, Yiva was abusive, but management struggled to get rid of her. Go figure.

After that turn of events, I decided I wouldn't be at that job much longer. I no longer desired to be in a place where I felt unappreciated. I will be honest; I was far from perfect. I was not equipped to implement certain protocols. Karmen had spent time rambling off certain protocols but not all of them. One night I was handed a protocol and completed it based on my interpretation. Though I fulfilled the task, I did not document it properly. And, in nursing, "If it is not documented, you didn't do it."

Karmen found out, told everybody, and eventually got around to telling me. Then, after discussing the issue with me, she followed up with an email to my bosses' boss and other educators, summarizing everything and framing it as inexcusable. Karmen did stuff like that frequently.

There are a few reasons Karmen did not appreciate my presence. First, she and a lot of the staff there were Filipino. From what I understood, that hospital recruited many nurses from the Philippines almost a decade prior. The hospital paid for their visas, and an exchange was able to underpay them. That hospital was their livelihood, and they took their work very seriously. It was likely because they had to dedicate years of their lives to the organization. The Filipinos had experienced a lot together, so they stood up for each other in a sibling-like fashion. Many of them had left their families in the Philippines, so they only had each other. They hung out before and after work, knew each other's children, and went to parties together. When new people arrived at the unit, they had to protect each other. Karmen seemed to be their leader, possibly because she held a position of authority. I recall one of the Filipino nurses backing a young white nurse in a corner and threatening her. The event wasn't discussed, which is weird because gossip usually spread like wildfire at that hospital. I realized that if Karmen wanted situations to be under the rug, that's where they stayed. I do not believe there were any consequences for that nurse.

Despite the toxic environment at that hospital, I had the opportunity to meet new people. Mixed in all the chaos were some great nurses like Kasey. Kasey was a driven individual. Her goal was to go back to her home country and build an entire hospital. She wanted to understand American hospitals and replicate them back home to care for her family. How amazing is that?

I also met Nancy, a sweet white woman who was well-traveled and had recently married. She was in love, and her focus was her husband. She had some challenging nights on the unit, but we did it together.

Then, there was Tameka. Tameka and I connected, and I am not sure why. She had a daughter who was only a few months old, and my youngest was about two years older. We had a lot of experiences in the unit and shared our life stories. We would sit in my office and talk for hours. She was even a pivotal part of my journey while writing this book. Tameka is of Jamaican descent, first-generation. She's fiery, loud, intentional, loving, driven, and self-aware. She is one of the few people I have ever met who knows how to listen intently. I have learned throughout my life that many people cannot truly listen beyond words. Most people are so focused on themselves that they don't have the space to receive what is given. Have you ever waited for your turn to speak while conversing with someone? Well, that means you were not listening. Instead, you were thinking about your response. Most people live in that realm. Tameka was able to listen, so she stood out to me.

These amazing nurses that I have mentioned no longer work at that hospital. They all agreed it was not an environment they wanted to engage in long-term. When they'd had enough of the toxicity, they moved on. So did I.

I was exhausted, stressed, and being bullied. I had two daughters and a disabled husband. When I realized how harmful the environment was to my well-being, I knew I had to do something different. Desperate, I began looking for jobs. I still wanted to work in professional development, but those jobs were few and far. I perused Indeed regularly and eventually started directly emailing people I knew could hire me. I explored all types of healthcare jobs, hoping to find a leadership position.

One Sunday, while my husband grilled, I searched Google for hospital leadership email addresses. I looked up anyone listed on a hospital's website as leadership. After finding the email address of the VP of quality for a 14-hospital system, I decided to shoot my shot. Surprisingly, she emailed me back and invited me to interview with her and two of her directors.

When I went into that interview, I was nervous

as hell, but I made sure I was cute. I didn't want my hair to be why I didn't land the job, so I ensured it was tucked tightly. Did I ever imagine working in a corporate environment? Absolutely not. As a nurse, when protocols or operations change, we would ask why, and the response was always, "Corporate told us to do it." During my interview, I sat with the people who made the decisions. I couldn't believe it.

I guess I sold myself well because they hired me. I told them that my experience was not as extensive as the position I received and informed them I would need help and support. They appeared to be understanding, supportive, and willing to work with me. They paid for the training I needed, and the next thing I knew, I was making 120K annually. That was a magical moment for me.

In addition to making more than I had ever made in my life, the job gave me experience equivalent to a master's degree in hospital business. When I walked away, I knew I would be equipped with knowledge of the business side of hospital systems. Regardless of everything else I experienced, the job gave me a solid foundation. I learned processes, mapping, priorities, building visions, planning, and more.

One of my projects was to save $1.4 million by conserving stents. That goal was unachievable. We asked how $1.4 million was defined for us to achieve, and they stated, "We take 7% off the top." There was no consideration of the actual cost of stents or the volume of cents for each hospital. Nothing is just "7% off the top."

I was eventually asked to help facilitate using a different company for stents. However, the quality of those stents had not been supported by evidence. In addition, one hospital couldn't do imaging because of the material the stents were made of. Nevertheless, corporate was determined to take this route because it was a cheaper option and had the potential to help us save $1.4 million. That was my first major project, and there was a lot of pressure on me to conquer this irrational, unfeasible, and nearly impossible task. The doctors and I eventually came up with a clinically consistent and optimal plan that would also achieve some savings. I saved around 989K in stents.

I was often told that if I wanted to keep my job, I had to save nine times more than what my salary was worth. So despite being excited about my salary, I had the pressure of proving I was valuable. Those statements made me question my worth. It didn't help that I'd just left a toxic work environment where I felt the same way. I felt like a little fish in a huge pond. Sometimes I was requested to do things against my ethical values, but I rationalized it by saying, "This is what I'm getting paid to do."

During my tenure at corporate, I was yelled at, belittled in public, and asked to work all types of hours. Once, when I had the flu, I was told that I was sick too often and even experienced discrimination, harassment, and retaliation based on the use of family and medical leave. I remember getting yelled at in a meeting because my numbers didn't make sense. When I went to talk to my boss, she said, "You'll get used to it. You need to present your numbers better."

I felt like I was always given impossible projects. The projects did not gather or garner support from my boss or anyone above him. Some large-scale projects should be implemented from the top-down. However, they often preferred a bottom-up approach, and I was responsible for driving it upward.

Worse, due to external factors that I'll share later, I also experienced stress-induced insomnia. I was permitted to take FMLA to recover, but experienced retaliation from my boss upon my return. I was asked to adhere to deadlines defined before my FMLA, and my workload was doubled. A colleague experienced similar feelings of stress, but when she expressed it, she was removed from some of her responsibilities. I, on the other hand, was completely ignored.

On a lighter note, I learned and accomplished a lot in my two years there. I also met some interesting personalities I won't soon forget. For example, I had the pleasure of encountering Demi, who was magical. She was terrific at what she did and showed me the ropes initially. Prior to her role at corporate, Demi had a lot of experiences that helped her facilitate large groups in large projects. She was a wealth of knowledge. Demi had a hard life but always stayed in good spirits. She was always happy when you saw her. Demi's hearty laugh was infectious, and being in her presence was always a joy.

Then, there was Brad, a weird man who loved ice cream and fatty foods. He wanted to climb the corporate ladder but refused to say so. He was actually a stellar emergency room nurse and an adrenaline junkie. So, I'm sure he knew that sitting in meetings, explaining numbers, and debating facts wouldn't make him happy. Brad was okay with working 12 hours because he had just divorced his wife, his son was a teenager, and the only other thing he had was his Jeep. I loved Brad's Jeep. He sucked up to everyone except me. I guess he knew I wouldn't take him where he needed to go. Nevertheless, we had some great conversations.

There was also Katie, an Ivy League graduate. I couldn't believe I worked next to someone who probably had hundreds of thousands in debt for their Ivy League degree while I worked my ass off to pay off my city college degree and had very little credentials. I always got a kick out of that. Like Brad, Katie was weird. She had rabbits in her backyard and would catch, cook, and eat them for lunch. It was so strange to me. Anyway, Katie went through a lot during our time as coworkers. She had her first baby while her husband was in a doctoral program. I could see she was experiencing postpartum depression, but she never acknowledged it. I often heard her crying as she hid behind a curtain, claiming she was pumping milk. The job required many hours from us, which meant she was not spending those hours with her daughter. I felt sorry for her. To make matters worse, she was jumped. Shortly after this incident, she quit and moved to a small town in Virginia with her baby.

The last person I'll mention is Christine. Everyone on my team was white, and she was no different, except she had biracial children. Christine and I had a lot in common. We watched a lot of the same shows and loved candles. We even went to see a Red Man and Method Man performance together. I thought we were friends, but as I look back, our relationship was very superficial. Nevertheless, she was important to me because I needed connection while working that demanding job at corporate.

Despite the money I made, the fantastic personalities I encountered, and the experience I gained, I knew I could not stay at that job. So in November 2019, I walked away, determined to make more magic of my own with all the new tools I had acquired. I didn't know what the future would look like, but I wasn't afraid to jump off the ledge to find out.

Part Five

TEMPERANCE

"Get grounded and you will find the flow."

M eet Temperance. She is equally masculine and feminine. She stands on both earth and water and has complete control over the energy flow between her cups. She stands strong and finds joy on earth. She doesn't need anyone to entertain her; everything is before her. Her independence attracts both intrigue and envy. She's focused and intentional. If she allowed her mind to wander, she would lose her balance and drop the cups along with her power.

There is so much we could learn from Temperance. In today's society, we give much of our attention to outside sources. We feed our minds with mindlessness and allow it to drive our daily actions. We never consider the purpose of our actions. We form opinions based on someone else's opinion without even checking for validity. We repeat memes as if we have researched the topic ourselves. We don't realize that we hold the power of our lives. Instead, we allow others to make decisions for us. We debate fake concepts and cancel people with no consideration of their humanity. Unlike Temperance, we struggle to find our flow and the energy to focus our thoughts.

Meditation appears intimidating to most, but it is incredibly beneficial for maintaining balance. It allows us to reconnect with the source by shutting off input from the outside world. Meditation permits us to connect with our senses without judgment. It provides us with the opportunity to be present at the moment and become aware of ourselves — from head to toe and everything in between. Meditation ensures we make impactful decisions without dropping our cups...or power.

After ten years of being a nurse, I still allowed life to happen to me. When I was a little girl, my dad would tell me, "You have to go to school and be smart so you can make $45 an hour and not five dollars an hour." So I internalized that as the benchmark for success. When I surpassed that goal and made six figures, I felt lost. I didn't know what to do. I no longer had a goal.

Let's rewind a bit to October 2018. I had just quit the job where I was bullied and felt a bit damaged. Nevertheless, I was optimistic about my future. Not long after my departure, I accepted a new position and was permitted to choose my start date. Rather than start work immediately as I'd done in the past, I decided to give myself three weeks and a half off. My start date at my new job was planned for November 2018. After feeling helpless for eight months, allowing myself to rest before taking on the new job was empowering. Also, I needed time to become accustomed to sleeping at night again.

Three weeks of vacation? I didn't know what to do with myself. In my entire adulthood, I had only taken a break that long when Madisyn was born. I only knew how to work, sleep, and take care of the kids. I had to find an activity to keep myself busy, so I decided to start going to the gym. I did a free consultation to set goals and learn which gym equipment suited my body type. I followed through on the goals and felt great. I tried everything: cycling, Zumba, and even yoga.

In addition to the gym, I planned my first Halloween party, a wine tasting. We invited a wine connoisseur to educate us on the different wines, my mom made a cake in the shape of a skull, and we had different types of candy to pair with the wines. It was a good time filled with laughter, jokes, and fellowship.

This may sound a little bizarre, but the world began to appear differently to me. The trees were more beautiful than they had ever looked before. Around that time, it was fall, and the leaves seemed to glow in the most breath-taking shades of amber and gold. During those three weeks, I found a deeper appreciation for things I couldn't do before, like meeting Madisyn at the bus stop. As parents, we often overlook the smallest moments with our little ones. We don't realize those moments are fleeting until they are moments of the past. Then, we look at our children and wonder, "Where has the time flown?" My vacation made me keenly aware that time was passing and would never return.

One day, I decided to take my daughters to the playground, and my cousin joined us. At that time, my youngest was three, and Madisyn was eight. As Madisyn ran, played, and jumped around, I put my little one on the swing and rocked her back-and-forth while my cousin and I discussed life. We were both in transitions. She was going through a divorce, and I was transitioning into a new career role. As we dreamed about what the future had in store for us, I blurted out, "I want to visit Hawaii."

At the time, my vacation time was nearly done. It made me realize that three weeks is a very short time frame. I told my cousin that if I traveled to Hawaii, I would stay for two weeks. She looked at me and asked, "How will you stay in Hawaii for two weeks? That sounds expensive."

"I don't know," I replied. "But, I'll figure it out."

I called my cousin, Pamela, who was stationed in Hawaii, to see if she would be willing to have us. She was delighted to have us as her guests. I asked my sister to join us, and she agreed. My sister was a single professional woman at the time. She loved to travel and had nothing to restrain her from doing so.

I went into my new job knowing that I would go to Hawaii as soon as I could take my vacation. We had to wait six months to take vacation time, which meant I accumulated Paid Time Off (PTO) for six months. I nearly had two weeks of vacation time when we were ready to go. As for the new habits I'd developed during my vacation, I worked hard to maintain them. On Mondays, I still went to yoga after work. I refused to let yoga go. I would leave work about 15 minutes earlier to make it to the yoga class on time. That was my way of taking my life back. I yearned to be like Temperance, but I was nowhere near discovering the balance, peace, or power to find flow.

Taking on a new job is exciting. Well, at least for me. It's like the first day of school all over again. You get to meet new people. You have butterflies in your stomach as you are unsure of what to expect. You wonder what work will be like and how your peers will treat you. At that point in my life, I considered myself a professional job starter. In 2018 alone, I had three different jobs. I was excited about my fourth new job because I had finally reached the top. However, I also knew that I was at the bottom of the top, so I had a ladder to climb. I was determined to understand how to climb that ladder.

The first six months at my new job were a whirlwind

of learning and absorbing the culture and processes I was responsible for improving. I was a little fish in a huge pond and had not yet harnessed my ability to sell myself to people. If I knew then what I know now, I would have sold myself initially. Instead, I got nervous when speaking to new people. I didn't know where people fit in the organization's dynamic, so I was very cautious. When it is your job to insert yourself into 14 organizations, knowing where everyone fits is vital. Over time, I became overwhelmed, but I always did as I was told.

My vacation to Hawaii couldn't have come at a better time. After six months of getting acclimated to new environments, I was desperate for a break. Visiting Hawaii was a new adventure, and I refused to be stressed out. I had taken three or four-day vacations in the past, but that trip was different — I was taking my entire family to Hawaii for two weeks. Leading up to my vacation, I received feedback from others that made me doubt the trip. "Why would you take a three-year-old to Hawaii? Isn't that expensive? How can you afford that?" The criticism was seemingly endless. During that time, I learned that my closest social network typically commented on my decisions by inserting their fears into my experience. Realizing this taught me when to listen and when to disengage. I decided not to worry about others' responsibilities or concerns. I fought hard to keep myself together on my new journey and was determined to stay inflow like Temperance.

Hawaii was full of excitement. The weather was perfect and beautiful. It felt good to be there, and Pamela was a lovely host. She is seven years younger than me and possesses a light that she has maintained through some of the most challenging times. When we were children, Pamela had a way of finding beauty in the smallest details, and she carried that into her adulthood.

These two weeks were crucial for me. It proved that I could do something different and exciting for myself. It was also vital for Pamela to have us there. A few weeks before our arrival, her mother, my Aunt Paige, passed away.

Aunt Paige was the reason my younger cousin shined so brightly. Many people didn't realize how much Aunt Paige's death cut through me, mostly because I don't approach death like most people. Before she died, my dad called to inform me she had suffered a stroke. She was found outside my grandmother's house and taken to the hospital. When my dad called, she was still alive, talking, and in good spirits. Unfortunately, Aunt Paige had been sick for a long time. So, despite the excellent report, I knew that I would probably never see her alive again after the stroke.

Aunt Paige spent quite a bit of time in the hospital. I refused to hear about her condition because there was nothing I could do to help her. She lived in Florida, and I lived in Maryland. I also chose not to speak to her, and I felt guilty after she died. My last memories were when she was full of life, rather than fearing death. I strived to keep my loved ones out of the "patient" category in my mind. After ten years of nursing, I witnessed many patients die and learned to find beauty in it. However, it is difficult to see the beauty in death when watching your loved ones take their last breath, listening to conversations ladened with fear, or hearing the signs of death rattle through their voices. This is one of the many reasons I believe ignorance is bliss.

On the day Aunt Paige died, I was driving home from work, and the strangest thing happened. Rain wasn't in the forecast, but hurricane-like weather came out of nowhere. There were huge raindrops, scary winds, and the sky was extremely dark. It only lasted for five minutes, but it happened at the exact time of Aunt Paige's death. It was so bad I had to pull the car over. At the time, I was worried about missing my yoga class and had not shed a tear about my aunt's death.

After the weather passed over, I proceeded to yoga class. Part of my yoga included meditation. I practiced Iyengar Yoga, so I was usually completely cleansed by the end of my practice. I noticed a new person in class that day. She was an older black lady with ample bosoms. I took a mental note of her presence but went on about my practice as usual. As soon as I left my class, the tears broke free. My sobbing was so uncontrollable I couldn't walk. The older black lady with the bosoms grabbed me, and I told her all about my guilt for not visiting my aunt or talking to her. She told me that my aunt knew exactly what I had to say to her. Then, she grabbed me and hugged me within her large bosoms. That woman held me until I regained my strength. I thanked her a million times, and she responded as if that was something she did for everyone all the time. I walked away from that encounter feeling protected.

Aunt Paige was important to me because she accepted me. She didn't judge me, and she was the first person I knew who openly embraced her blackness. Aunt Paige let her flaws hang freely. She was unapologetic about letting the world see them. Though she had a hard life, Aunt Paige saw the sunshine in every dark cloud. She gave me a perspective about life that I cherish to this day. It was vital for me to experience Aunt Paige in my youth, and I am forever grateful I knew her.

The hurt I experienced from her death was insurmountable. I'm sure you can imagine the grief was ten times worse for her children. Although my trip to Hawaii originated from my desire to be free, it allowed me to reconnect with my cousin, and therefore, reconnect with my aunt. Though she rarely showed it during our visit, I knew Pamela was in pain. I am grateful that my family was able to bring life into her home and give her a reason to laugh and smile.

As I said before, Pamela was an amazing host and showed us a great time. In addition to all the must-see tourist spots, she also took us to the places the locals enjoyed. We jumped off the cliffs, hiked in the rainforest, camped on the beach, went paddle boating, ate at food trucks, and saw a wholphin. Yes, I meant a wholphin. A whale/dolphin. It's real; look it up.

Hawaii was a memorable trip. It allowed me to become one with the earth, experience adventure, and tap into my inner Temperance. Hawaii was my first step to finding my flow, and there was way more work to be done.

Part Six

THE CHARIOT

"Take a risk. A big one. Even after you failed at full speed."

When you're unfamiliar with the flow of life, flow can seem scary until you find the rhythm behind the flow. The Chariot reminds us to be fearless, stand tall, take action with the life lessons bestowed upon us, and move forward. The Chariot is pulled by two sphinxes going in different directions, and though he has no reigns to redirect them, he does not worry. The charioteer knows that his true strength lies in his will and mind. With focus and determination, he knows he can direct them forward. So, throw on your leather jacket, put on your crown, and remember you are protected. You still hold your magic wand, and you can create all the magic you need.

After our marvelous adventure in Hawaii, I had to return to a life that was far from the one I'd imagined for myself. My family is my top priority, I had to consider them before making any decisions, but something was pushing me to take a risk and be adventurous. Hawaii had left me with a high I didn't just want for two weeks every year. I wanted every day of my life to be an adventure. When I woke up in the morning, I longed to be excited about the day ahead. However, when you work five days a week, the days become monotonous. The same daily exercises and tasks eventually begin to lull you to sleep. You know what to expect from everyone because you deal with them every day. Before you know it, you succumb to a humdrum lifestyle and begin to accept things that were once unacceptable. That was my life, and once again, I decided to do something different.

According to the US Bureau of Labor Statistics, about 20% of small businesses fail within the first year. The average length of a successful business is about 20 years, and by ten years, only about a third of businesses survive. Additionally, after five years, 50% of businesses falter. I was one of the 20% that failed within the first year. My first business, The Yogi Journey, failed due to a lack of cash flow. As I write this book, I am in the third year of running my second business, Cannabis Nursing Solutions™.

Cannabis Nursing Solutions™ began shortly after the short-lived experience called The Yogi Journey. My first experience with yoga was surreal. I noticed my eyeballs for the first time in a while, my hips were tight, and the downward dog was a joke. I was one of the few black women in the room and the youngest, so I felt like I was being watched. I committed to learning about yoga and ultimately relearning how to move my body. Walking, sitting, and listening became different. I learned how to receive the world through senses I had ignored because of my focus on the outside world.

Ironically, the gym I attended is associated with one of the hospitals I worked for, and I only used the membership after I quit. At first, I had flashbacks of when I was bullied at that employment. However, in true Ashley fashion, I have reclaimed that place as a sanctuary. I see it as where I learned to experience the world again. That gym is the reason why I recovered from the bullying situation. It is how I learned that there is more than what is perceived through your environment. Every time I attend a yoga class, I approach the gym in gratitude.

Fueled by a desire to show the utmost gratitude to yoga, I began The Yogi Journey. At the time, all I had was my work experience, and I was still new to my performance improvement job. Nevertheless, I was thrilled and determined that it would be the experience I needed to become rich. I had also begun learning about the universal laws, which included the law of attraction, the law of karma, etc. Like many new to learning about universal laws, I assumed money would just float to me.

During that time, I committed to learning more about financial management. I listened to podcasts and read books like Rich Dad Poor Dad. The author of Rich Dad Poor Dad says there are three ways to increase your earning potential: real estate, stocks, or entrepreneurship. He suggests optimizing it by doing all three. So, I decided to take a shot at entrepreneurship first. I knew some absolute idiots who owned businesses, so I figured, "Why can't I?"

Well, entrepreneurship is hard, and those idiots aren't idiots. A lot goes into entrepreneurship, and The Yogi Journey only scratched the surface. Being an entrepreneur is especially difficult if your immediate social circle does not embrace entrepreneurship. I learned early on that my social circle would provide insight from fear-based perspectives, so I had to go against everything I knew to try entrepreneurship. I bought a website domain, figured out WordPress, researched blogging, and created graphics for shirts. Let's just say it was a fun and an expensive hobby.

The experience was not totally in vain, though. I learned about websites. I learned about domains. I learned not to hire virtual assistants (VA's) until processes are in place. And I realized that I had to have brand awareness for my graphics to sell, and my audience needed to flow through the whole funnel. There were a lot of lessons learned and, in my opinion, perfectly aligned for what was to come.

Slowly, I stopped dedicating so much time to The Yogi Journey. I remained faithful to yoga, but I stopped taking pictures for IG and blogging. I knew I had to do something different but was unsure what to do. I wanted to offer a service and be an expert at something. I loved yoga but was not an expert. I was just documenting my journey. I could not do those cool moves that drew attention. My highest-level move was the crow pose. After that, I was done. I knew I would not attract an audience based on that alone. Also, I did not want to be a yoga instructor. It was not my calling.

One evening, after a long and exhausting day at work, I felt a bit down on myself. My mind raced, and I could not sleep. My husband, on the other hand, snored all night long. I tried to "accidentally" wake him up but was unsuccessful. So, I did what any other working mom does in the middle of the night: I scrolled Facebook.

While scrolling, I found a course about cannabis taught by a fellow nurse. It offered contact hours, which I was fond of, so I registered on a whim. On December 1, 2017, Maryland's Medical Marijuana Program went live after a five-year delay. In October 2018, I traveled to Los Angeles to attend a training course about medical marijuana. That was only a few months after my trip to Hawaii, so I used my last bit of PTO to take the trip.

That was the first time the class was being offered.

Even though there were a lot of processes that needed to be implemented, the course was offered at a significant discount. As a part of the first cohort, I only paid $500 to attend. It included lunch, and I met a cool colleague who became a significant connection in the cannabis nurse space.

That trip to LA was the first personal vacation I had ever taken, and it was exhilarating. One of my long-time girlfriends lived in LA, so I stayed with her and her brother. On the day of the course, I got up before sunrise, caught a bus, then an uber, and made it to downtown LA safely. When I arrived, the facility was beautiful. I was very excited about the information I learned and could not wait to take it back to Maryland.

I decided to go to happy hour with the trainer and thought we connected. However, the thing about a salesman is that they are always selling. We talked for hours about husbands, nursing, jobs, etc. We were out so long, my girlfriend got worried because we were supposed to see a movie that evening. In the midst of us chatting away, I finally noticed my friend's call, so I wrapped it up, jumped on the bus, and took the uber back to my girlfriend's house. Long story short, that was one of the best trips of my life.

When I returned to Maryland, I started Cannabis Nursing Solutions™ immediately. I wanted to be the source of all solutions in Cannabis Nursing. At the time, I knew (or thought I knew) that the information I had was innovative. I was focused. The entire time was a bit of a blur because I was so intent on organizing the content. As I reflect, I was in the same state of mind as when I wrote this book. The only thing I could think about was the content, and I spent all of my free time working on it. I wanted it to be organized so I could implement it during consultations, but there was so much information to consider. There is no way to walk away with information about the plant and think you know everything. Organizing the content allowed me to absorb and own what I learned. Once organized, I decided that it could be a training course, and that is how I eventually created the Cannabis Nursing Solutions™ Training course. The intention was to train nurses in hospital settings during orientation or as a competency.

All nurses should be competent in Cannabinoid Therapy, but I did not anticipate how large the stigma is in the larger context of the collective thought. While creating my training course, I met another nurse in Maryland who identified as a Cannabis Nurse, and we scheduled a time to meet up. I thought our meet-up would just be the two of us, but she brought along other nurses. I did not know what to expect from this group but was very interested in what they had to say. One nurse broke down in tears explaining how she chose the plant, but her husband did not approve because of the differences in income. Their stories and experiences gave me much-needed insight into the cannabis industry. I learned that many nurses who entered the industry early have a strong emotional connection with the plant, and emotions always cloud judgment. So I strived to be clear about why cannabis was important to me. Cannabis represents freedom. Like yoga, cannabis medicine introduced me to another way of thinking about healthcare.

In health care, many nurses are oppressed. The concept of oppression can be triggering for many, especially those of us of color, but hear me out. How were you indoctrinated into the nursing profession? I spent time as an instructor. When asked why they wanted to be a nurse, many first-semester students responded with some traumatic story of a family member they witnessed in the hospital, a childhood disease, or carrying on a legacy. In many respects, that question is harmless. It is necessary to identify the purpose behind everything we do. However, many of our reasons for pursuing nursing are tied to emotional needs we've conjured, so we feel forced to accept the constraints assigned to nursing to satiate those emotional needs.

Once we enter the nursing profession, reality hits. We realize that the rules and policies are set and defined. Our job is to follow them, no matter how outdated or inapplicable to a specific scenario they may be. Refusing to follow the rules results in a write-up or our licenses being on the line. In our earliest days in nursing school, we are taught which answer is the priority. It did not matter if our mind rationalized another response or considered other factors; the priority is just priority based on some arbitrary set of constraints that we may or may not be aware of. With that being said, our drive to not turn our backs on this experience has led us to feel oppressed. Nurses tend to be type-A personalities because we are conditioned to see a scenario in every patient. We don't always see the patient as a human. Once I became aware of this in my practice, it became difficult to be satisfied with the status quo. "Who is making the decisions? How do they decide? Who was in the room when it happened?" *In the words of Hamilton.....*

No one else was in the room where it happened
The room where it happened
The room where it happened
No one else was in the room where it happened
The room where it happened
The room where it happened
No one really knows how the game is played
The art of the trade
How the sausage gets made
We just assume that it happens
But no one else is in the room where it happens

All types of questions intruded on my mind.

When I learned about cannabis, I was intrigued by the possibility of alternative ways to help people heal. There was a possibility that I could walk into the industry from an evolved perspective and create the Cannabis Nurse Industry based on new constructs and new rules. That level of freedom is a part of my calling as a human. As I spent more time as an Endocannabinoid Specialty™ Nurse, I saw that same emotion evoked related to cannabis because of the healing it provided for many. However, it has equally caused a lot of hurt for those in the War on Drugs in Prohibition. So, yes. I love the plant as much as anyone else. But my love is due to the freedom it provides nurses and employing other perspectives in healthcare that would otherwise be inexistent.

So...back to the meeting...

That meeting revealed that there are more nurses like me, but none of them had pigmented skin like me. The only other time I was the only woman of color on a team was at my last job. That experience at my previous job caused me to be extremely cautious with that group of nurses. The worry of being retaliated against was real, but I knew I needed a tribe, so I tried to stay connected.

After our meeting, I reached out via email, hoping we could meet up regularly. It never went anywhere. Nobody answered my emails until *Asa's Medicine* was published, so I was alone trying to make my way in this undefined sea called the Cannabis Industry.

In September 2019, I got contact hours assigned to my training course and started educating. I would occasionally hold the training courses on my days off from work. Nobody came to my first training course, but I knew I had to keep going. Every time I wanted to quit, someone would reach out to ask how the training course was going, how to attend the course, or to point me in the direction of a lead. Every. Single. Time.

I occasionally talked to my colleague, who offered a bit of comfort, but she was down south, and I was in Maryland. So the comfort only went so far. In the early days of Cannabis Nursing Solutions™, we would talk for hours about the struggles of being a Cannabis Nurse. With no accurate guidance, we would chat about the dead ends, the stigma, feeling lost, events, and so much more. We both felt alone; until we did not. She went to the American Cannabis Nurses Association (ACNA) Conference in 2019 and met more nurses like us. Some were black and brown like us, and she was excited to share this with me. During that conference, she also learned that there was a Cannabis Nursing Handbook in the works. That handbook was intended to guide nursing schools when they were ready to implement Cannabis Nursing into schools, which, on the surface, appeared to be a giant leap forward for nurses.

I also learned about the National Council for State Boards of Nursing (NCSBN) Guidelines, which discuss the seven principles of nursing care for the Medical Cannabis Patient. The seven principles require the nurse to:

- Know the current state of legalization of medical and recreational cannabis use
- Know the principles of a Medical Marijuana Program
- Have a general understanding of the endocannabinoid system, cannabinoid receptors, cannabinoids, and the interactions between them
- Have an understanding of cannabis pharmacology and the research associated with the medical use of cannabis
- identify the safety considerations for patient use of cannabis
- Have no judgment regarding the patient's choice of treatment or preferences in managing pain and other distressing symptoms
- be aware of medical marijuana administration considerations

NCSBN is the overarching council that guides the local state boards of nursing. They are also responsible for the National Council Licensure Examination (NCLEX), a state licensure test every nurse must pass to become a Registered Nurse (RN). The test's methodology is reviewed annually for improvements. In 2008, older nurses would say, "I remember when the test was on paper." As for me, I recall when the "select all that can apply" questions were the most challenging to answer. Now, there are more interactive questions, and test-takers have to label images and more.

Anyway, NCSBN developed the guidelines in 2018. I wrote this book in 2021, and many of our state boards did not guide local facilities on the need for Cannabinoid Education. The average nurse is unaware of the guiding principles and practice under the stigma that is perpetuated throughout nursing schools. The general message in schools is that cannabis is bad. According to a study shared at an ACNA meeting, only 7% agree that their nursing school educates students on managing patients using medicinal cannabis. This study had 1,500 participants. There are no discussions on plant anatomy, the endocannabinoid system, or even, at minimum, the recent evolution of the laws and legislation. I remember listening to a lawyer discuss these guidelines, and I distinctly noted that as the lawyer for NCSBN, her job is to protect that entity. It is not her job to protect the nurses who follow the organizations' guidelines.

With all of that evolving over a few years, I realized the Endocannabinoid Specialty™ Nurse would eventually be a big deal. The foundations were being built right before my eyes. As I observed the key players create a major impact in an industry that had yet to be defined, I was mind-blown. Nobody referred to us as an Endocannabinoid Specialty ™ Nurse until I created my line of shirts. We generally and affectionately call ourselves Cannabis Nurses, but we are not Cannabis Nurses. We serve the need for a balanced endocannabinoid system. Thus, our specialty is the endocannabinoid system. Comparable to a Cardiac Nurse, not a Cardizem Nurse. (Only fellow nurses will get that reference.)

Anyway, let's get back to the key players. They created organizations, and following that — I am not even sure they realize how beautiful it is — created collective thought and drove missions forward. I knew it was not my job to do that piece. I hadn't defined my role yet, but I felt like I was somehow the glue, providing solutions to my colleagues as they moved their missions forward.

There were times when I got concerned about the interpretation of cannabis medicine. Cannabis medicine is an option, not an answer. Cannabis can be a tool in healing, but it is not a crutch. It does not cure. It is not to be mixed with other herbs without an expert. It is a plant. It has genetic components that mimic cannabinoids that we also produce called endocannabinoids. Many of us are deficient and simply need to jumpstart our endocannabinoid system to take steps toward wellness. It is not intended for overindulgence. In fact, in the case of overindulgence, its ability to relieve symptoms is significantly lowered. A therapeutic window can only be found if used intentionally and with precision.

Unfortunately, that is not the message communicated at large. Instead, it's almost as if cannabidiol (CBD) is the cure for everything. However, CBD is from the same plant as Tetrahydrocannabinol (THC). You can buy CBD anywhere. The person who sells Herbalife also sells CBD. The person who classifies cannabis as Sativa without mentioning the terpene profile and cannabinoid composition has no idea what they are selling you. And no, it is not just weed.

Those misconceptions justified the need for an endocannabinoid specialist. We need specialists that consider all aspects of a person's relation to the world and support patients in becoming the best versions of themselves by considering cannabis and making doable lifestyle changes like eating healthier, walking, intimacy, massage therapy, and so much more. These are many of the reasons why our mission at Cannabis Nursing Solutions™ is to shift the perspectives in healthcare by empowering healthcare providers to become change agents through solutions that are inclusive of spiritual, mental and holistic healing practices. We aim to provide awareness of the evolution of healthcare through books and speaking engagements; while providing healthcare providers with the support they need through training, coaching, networking and various opportunities to achieve their personal and entrepreneurial goals. This allows us to offer a distinct service that utilizes the Nursing Process, Individualized Treatment Care Plans, and a method of evaluating progress in the continuum of care for our patients. We provide strategies to patients seeking alternative and holistic solutions to manage chronic illness. We educate, empower, and assist patients on their journey to safely utilize medical cannabis to bring them back to oneness.

Unfortunately, as a nurse, we often do not consider these options. We are often overworked, overburdened, and rarely considered experts, so we cannot open our awareness beyond the next pill or whose bladder to empty next. That was a larger problem that needed a larger solution, but in the meantime, I began preparing my personal life for what seemed like an exciting, new adventure.

Part Seven

THE WHEEL OF FORTUNE

"What goes up must come down. But what goes down must also come up."

I f we step back and expand our view like a telescope viewing the earth, we will notice that there is stability, even in moments of chaos. The Wheel of Fortune gives us an aerial view. As the wheel spins, our view changes as our position shifts up and down. No matter our position on the wheel, our tools continue to be at arm's reach. However, we may not see them all depending on our current viewpoint. That doesn't mean they aren't all there. Our minds may choose to panic, but we must observe our position and ride the wave. When we think of the Wheel of Fortune, the game show might come to mind. We may immediately assume that fortune is on its way and be cautious not to let it slip through our fingers. The truth is, fortune is always on its way, but are you ready for it?

Time and space are relative. Here and now is an experience. The Wheel of Fortune represents all the dimensions and lets us know that our fortune awaits us. But what is fortune? Is it money? Or, is it more than that? I believe it is more, but let's stick with the money. Money is simply energy, and our mindsets attract that energy when it is aligned with it. Money energy ebbs and flows just like all other energy; there is a natural rhythm to all things. When the wheel shifts, how we align with our opportunities to attract money shifts.

In 2020, according to the Internet Crimes Report, approximately 800,000 Internet crimes were reported. Many people believe that Internet crimes are specific to older adults because of the preconceived notion that they are the most vulnerable. In 2020, approximately 105,000 adults over 60 were victims of Internet crimes. Additionally, 179,000 victims were between the ages of 30 and 50, which means middle-aged adults are actually more vulnerable to attacks.

Of the 800,000 Internet crimes reported, approximately 28,000 people reported experiencing a spoofing attack. Spoofing is a form of cyberattack. It is a crime where a scammer disguises themselves as a trusted person. Generally, the targeted people are older adults or people in highly vulnerable situations. Based on the statistics, Internet crimes do not seem to be very prevalent, and even less prevalent are people who report spoofing attacks. As the victim of a spoofing attack, I know how difficult it can be to report something intangible and not likely to be resolved.

My husband and I began our house search in December 2018. I had already decided that Cannabis Nursing Solutions™ would be the source of my income, so I began planning as if it were so. I decided that there would be a period when I would not have a traditional job, so I wanted to make sure that would not be a barrier to getting a larger home. My youngest daughter was almost a toddler, and our first home was not intended for an expanding family.

By the end of December, we found a foreclosure that needed work, so it was under market value. I believed that was the house for us because it was an easy find. It took us less than two weeks to discover it. We had a supportive team throughout the process. Our realtor was amazing, and so was our broker. I always recommend people to find a team they can trust in all their adventures. When things go well, it's not as important, but when they don't, having a good team is everything. We could not have foreseen the trickery people can do in this digital age, but I'm grateful we had a good team along for the journey.

Someone in Venezuela mimicked my real-estate agent, broker, and their assistants' email addresses. In the beginning, they would email as if they were my real estate agent, my broker, and their assistants. We had a general conversation, and they seemed to know everything about our plans to close. They emailed me for weeks, and when we got close to our closing date, they sent instructions on how to send the down payment. Our down payment was a little higher considering the price of the home. We were getting a renovation loan, so I wanted our mortgage payments to be lower.

There were some red flags that many would have overlooked. In the final days, the emails were slightly pushy, considering the personality archetypes of our team. Also, when we spoke to our team in person, they did know what we had emailed about. I figured they forgot. Additionally, I ran into some difficulty sending the wire transfer where I had the chance to reconsider the bank account it was being sent to.

The day before closing, we went to do a final walk-through of the house with my realtor. I informed them that I had already sent the wire transfer, but she convinced me that sometimes it takes a while to appear in the account. She brushed it off, and so did I. I took off from work the next day because our closing appointment was at 9 AM. I always pay attention to the weather; it reflects my mood in many ways. On beautiful sunny days, I tend to be in good spirits, and on dark rainy days, my mood is glum. On our "closing day," the skies were cloudy and grey. I thought it was raining that day, but when my husband and I talked about it later, he said it didn't rain. It is funny how your mind can take an experience and make it fit your reality.

As we drove to our closing appointment, I received a phone call from our realtor asking about the funds for the down payment. At that moment, my heart dropped. I immediately knew something was wrong. The money was gone; I felt it. I was confused, concerned, and mad. I felt like a vulnerable child who had been mugged. Frustration raged through my entire body.

We were instructed to visit the bank to stop the wire transfer, but I had sent the transfer two days prior. So, the money had already been transferred. We went to our credit union and asked to speak with the manager. The manager and I knew each other from my time working there, so she immediately escorted us to her office. As I told her what happened, tears streamed down my face. She was devastated as well. She offered us encouraging words, but there was nothing she could do. Finally, she suggested we go to the receiving bank, so that's what we did.

When we arrived at that bank, it was crowded. There was a long line, and we were not customers. We finally got back to the manager's office and explained the situation. We learned that the bank was dedicated to its customers and would go to lengths to protect them. We didn't get any information. Devastated, lost, and directionless, we called our real estate agent. He was compassionate as well, but he stated, "I have been a real estate agent for over 20 years, and this is the first time this has ever happened to any of my clients." He was perplexed and had his team check the records and audit their software.

As we waited helplessly, my financial history ran through my mind. When I was in nursing school, I paid for my tuition out of pocket. First, I worked as a bank teller. Then, as I got closer to my graduation, I was qualified to work as a nurse tech at an acute rehab hospital for $16 an hour. That was the most I had ever made before. My jobs before those were mostly in foodservice. I had worked at Rita's Italian Ice, McDonald's, Ruby Tuesday, Red Lobster, and various other restaurants. When I finally got to work at the acute rehab hospital, I worked my ass off. I would work doubles, from 3 PM to 11 PM, then from 11 PM to 7 AM. If I had time, I would work double shifts five days a week to pay my tuition. I didn't want any debt. I lived with my parents at that time, so I did not have to pay rent. All my money went to my tuition, car insurance, and the little bit of fun I had when I wasn't at school or working.

My dad taught me to always save money, so I did. I was always saving for something. If I wanted an Xbox, I saved my money and bought an Xbox. If I wanted some shoes, I saved my money and purchased some shoes. I think my largest purchase as a young woman was my first car. It was a tan, 1993 Toyota Corolla, and I bought it from Aunt Paige for $500. Everything inside was manual. You had to crank the windows to roll them up and push the locks to lock the door, but I bought that car, and I loved it!

After moving out of my parents' house, I moved into an apartment with one of my good girlfriends. At that time, I was working as a nurse. I was able to cover my bills, but that's it. I had a little wiggle room, and of course, I still saved, but it wasn't enough to save $15,000. Then, Madisyn was born, we bought our first house with the help of NACA, we never put money down on our cars, our second daughter was born, and we had to splurge on unnecessary things we couldn't afford. Things were good. I'm not complaining. However, $15,000 wasn't available to my family. It was a lot of money.

In 2017, I had decided to do something different with my finances and create a real nest egg. I learned that most households don't have six months' worth of savings in their bank accounts to cover them in an emergency. As I thought about it, I realized that we should really have a year's worth of savings and made that the goal. We were very strategic about how we saved money. We didn't eat out as much, only bought things we needed, and put 10% of every paycheck in a separate bank account.

We saved more money than I had ever saved in my entire life. Then, in the blink of an eye, it was all gone. So many thoughts raced through my mind. Where will we live? How could someone do that? Am

I a good person? I lacked answers to every question in my mind, so they never went away. I told one of my coworkers what happened, and she told the rest of our coworkers. When I arrived at work the next Monday morning, all eyes were on me. I worked with one of the nicest, quirkiest, older women I had ever met named Doris. In her heyday, she was a hippie. I'm sure she smoked a lot of weed. Anyway, she had some of the best advice. She had no problem sharing wisdom with whoever needed to hear it. She never needed advice as she was too stuck in her ways, but I loved her.

When I walked into work that day, I walked into the biggest, warmest, and most compassionate hug I had ever felt in my life. As soon as Doris hugged me, I broke down in tears again. She was the first person to hug me since my life savings had been stolen. After that, a lot of people came by and told me they were sorry to hear about what happened. Once all that was over, I was expected to continue working as normal and then some. I came back to the same deadlines in place before my leave. I hit significant barriers with a couple of projects and was also asked to take on new projects. One of which was the implementation of the COPD and CHF pathways. Those were huge with no prioritization. That was also around the Children's Book Scandal that Mayor Pugh was eventually convicted of. Due to my recent theft, I was acutely aware of everything around me that was and was not said. It was chaos. I watched as many jobs were saved, and some were relinquished. I could not figure out how they determined who they would keep. There were whispers in meetings to which I had not been invited.

One afternoon after my coworker and I met about the timeline for the CHF Pathway, I remember my boss almost skipping down the hall. He told me he was excited because the Chief Improvement Officer had resigned, and he felt like he would get the job. I was confused because it had nothing to do with me, and I didn't understand why he assumed it would be his job. Even more puzzling, he seemed disgusted that I was not as excited that he would soon 'report to the CEO.' As I observed the shifts made to fix the optics, I continued to fulfill my responsibilities. It was never with a smile. I couldn't find the strength to whistle while I worked. I did what was asked of me, nothing more, nothing less.

One day, my boss told me he didn't think I was a good fit for the job anymore. He said my mood had changed, and I should look for something else within the system. Many events occurred, but he made some calls, found a job, and sent me text messages prompting me to make a choice. I could either take the job and make half of my current salary or be served with a Performance Improvement Plan (PIP).

That time reminded me of when I experienced postpartum depression. The world seemed so grey, and I felt alone and stupid. I constantly bombarded myself with questions I couldn't answer. I still felt as if somebody had beaten me up. No, the scam wasn't a physical assault, but it hurt just as bad. I felt it in my bones and muscles. When people asked how things were going, I struggled to answer with a smile. Many wanted to help me, and my real estate agent and broker sent money. The real estate agent's team also sent donations. Sadly, the money I received never replaced the $15,000 I lost. Nevertheless, I am grateful to the people who supported my family in such a difficult time.

In addition to the support we received, I also remember the support I didn't get. Our friends and family were the least compassionate. One family member stated, "Oh, wow! You should just be happy you had $15,000." Another said, "Oh, I didn't know you had $15,000! What did you do to get that?" My family didn't mean to be hurtful, but their comments wounded me badly. It didn't seem like they tried to understand the pain of my circumstance. To be honest, I knew that no one could understand that pain because it wasn't physical. It was spiritual.

What did I expect from them? I don't know. However, I did appreciate opportunities to talk about my pain without being projected on. The experience of losing $15,000 was haunting at best. My personal space had been invaded. I had an intruder that I couldn't see or touch. My mind could not wrap around that fact, and I needed help understanding how someone could do something so terrible. Eventually, I decided to accept it and move forward.

I began doing gratitude affirmations. In reality, I had a lot to be grateful for. First, I was grateful for Doris' unforgettable hug. Second, many people pitched in to help us, and we eventually got our house without selling the first house as we had initially planned. Third, my life had changed. My world was rocked. I no longer saw the world through the eyes of the girl who did not have $15,000 stolen from her. Through my gratitude affirmations, I learned about natural laws. One of the laws is cause-and-effect. I realized that if money could be taken from me that quickly and easily, I could attract it just as fast. And that is when the magic started to happen.

People know me to be resilient; I always keep it moving. Yes, I have intense moments, but I always know that I need to get back up. When life changes, we must adjust. I didn't want to change, but The Wheel of Fortune had already made its shift. I don't know your life condition, but if you are experiencing turmoil, know that you are also resilient. All you have to do is #KeepGoing. The Wheel of Fortune is always moving.

Part Eight

THE STAR

"In order to discover your value, you must first acknowledge your vulnerabilities."

W e are all the stars of our movies. Most of us just don't know it yet. It's funny how we can't see ourselves as stars, but we can idolize other humans who happen to be stars of movie productions. We put them on pedestals, obsess over their lives, and adopt their habits and choices as our own. We see them as superhumans when they are actually more exposed than we could ever stand to be. A movie star is simply a human portraying himself as a character in a leading role. What we see on screen is just a persona created in someone's mind, delivered through a screenplay, and brought to life by an actor.

The star has an integrated subconscious and conscious mind with intention and precision. They are experts at it. The star pours into us with their creativity, and their creativity can come in various forms. We place a high value on actors, actresses, musicians, and other forms of art, however, creativity can be demonstrated in many ways. Unfortunately, many of us do not recognize our own creative genuis, which is why we don't realize we are stars.

For quite some time, I suppressed what I had to offer. I did not believe I was a star. Along my journey of realizing my identity and worth, I learned that the world does not owe me validation of my skills. It is up to me to validate and protect myself. I had to learn that I was the star of my own story. I am the star of the show, and I am the main character. I always looked at myself as a supportive role in somebody else's story. As I shifted that perspective, I gained more control over the direction I was headed.

Working in various healthcare environments was highly stressful. Of course, no job is stress-free, but considering my experiences in healthcare, I decided that it would be easier not to be the star. Once you decide that you are not the star, you are officially "burned out."

Nursing burnout is a common term thrown around in hospitals. Hospitals are always trying to fix this problem to relieve the "nursing shortage." It is well known that nurses work in high-stress environments. According to the World Health Organization, burnout is a syndrome resulting from workplace stress. It is generally characterized by feelings of depression, exhaustion, and mental distance from their job, which reduces professional efficacy. Nurses experience physical and emotional fatigue related to the stressors of the long hours, quick decision-making, and the strain of caring for patients who have poor outcomes.

It does not take long before nurses become disengaged, cynical, or detached. It's not that we don't care about patients. We know that we are nurses and want to care for people. We know who we are supposed to be and how to keep our licenses. But we don't know how to get rid of the nagging feeling that something is not right. The world calls us heroes. We are supposed to be the stars of our own story, but we often find ourselves trapped in our thoughts.

At the point in my journey I will share in this chapter, I was slowly breaking through the trap of my thoughts. I decided to be a star in my own story and continued to work on Cannabis Nursing Solutions™. I had already transitioned out of that corporate position and into a job where I made half of my previous salary. I was burned out and exhausted. I knew working at that job wouldn't take me where I was supposed to go. On the other hand, entrepreneurship seemed to be getting me closer and closer to my purpose.

When my new boss asked me what my goals were for the year, my response would always be, "You tell me." By the time I got into my new role, I was no longer passionate about healthcare. At that point, I had been working in healthcare for more than 11 years, and it felt like I hadn't gone anywhere. I went from job to job, attempting to achieve something unachievable. I could not give my all to work anymore. I didn't verbalize this to my boss because I didn't have the words to share with her, but she was patient with me. In the last months of my employment at the hospital, I finally found the words and put them in this poem:

I love you. I hate you.

I hate you.
I hate that you force me to be somewhere
And I do not enjoy the vibrations.
I hate the people you surround me with
People who don't listen and do not appreciate love and light.
I hate that they are lost in habit
And not working on caring for the people they serve.
I hate that black girls like me are far and few between.
Why don't we know data, performance metrics, and hospital systems?
Damn
Not even meeting etiquette?
The role we serve is a microcosm in the system of healthcare.
So blind to the other roles
So busy fighting over being a Med/Surg nurse or an ICU nurse.
Really?

If that is what you are looking at
You are exactly what the system needs to remain complacent.
Black lives matter, right?
I hate just having to follow someone else's rules.
I have my own needs.
The hate I have for you goes beyond repair.
I have dedicated years of my life
Thinking I was going to serve and care for people
Only to learn that is not what actually happens.
We are forced to care for more people than our hearts can allow.
We are forced to turn off the love we have to offer.
I've watched time and time again,
Nurse after nurse, day after day
Their light is turned off by the trauma and disease.
When they start nursing school,
They ALL say the same thing;
I became a nurse because I love...
People
Helping
Advocating
Contributing to a healthier life
Ask them now...
I am a nurse because ....
Of the paycheck.
I am off four days a week.
I can become a manager and boss people around.

I can be better than the next nurse.

None of that builds on your purpose.

None of it builds on your soul.

You slowly turn the lights out and are left with the robots.

The ones who don't notice the bruises

The ones who carry the morphine in their pockets

The ones who left their children with who again?

Oh yes, their auntie.

But wait!

It's okay.

Because I AM a nurse,

But no longer a nurse.

I will ALWAYS be a nurse,

And, now, I am an author too!

I love you!

I love you because you watched me grow.

You watched a sheltered girl who saw very little of what life has to offer. You watched my girls be born.

You watched the postpartum depression take over and be overcome.

You watched me be bullied.

You watched my light dim with every year that passed.

You showed me nurses in all areas at various times in their careers.

I was a part of their development while I was developing too.

I love you because you stayed in my corner.
If I needed a job,
You had it for me.
Shoot, at one point, I had three of them.
I love you because I don't have student loans.
In fact, my first job gave me money just for being hired.
I love you because you have given me the opportunity to witness the cycle of life, time and time again.
I don't take it for granted.
I love you because someone took a chance on me
To teach me performance metrics, data, and hospital systems.
In this crazy world, I can see the system's structure.
I can see where I fit.
So I can move on with grace.
I love you because you provided for a young family that was not supposed to make it.
Ten years later, I can say we are making it and have big dreams.
So, thank you.
And now, it is time for you to grow up.
And it is my job to help.

Writing that poem helped me connect to the gratitude I felt towards healthcare and its impact on my life while acknowledging the hurt that came with what the system did to me. When I entered the healthcare arena, I was a naïve young girl, eyes glistening with hope and ready to change each patient with my touch. However, when reality hit, I realized that my impact wasn't significant enough. The system didn't allow my impact to be enough.

The new role that I took was called quality improvement coordinator. Daily, I looked at spreadsheets and made graphs for the units of the hospital. My position allowed me to see that much of hospitals' leadership didn't understand their metrics. Directors are paid bonuses when they achieve their metrics, but many didn't know how they impacted their metrics because they couldn't understand them. It was my job to help them. I was blown away when one leader asked me how to use Excel. I thought Excel proficiency was a fundamental skill for managers or directors. I guess I was wrong.

I went from being a hospital leader who didn't understand metrics to corporate, where everything was based on metrics, and then moved back into the hospital with a new perspective on data. I was very shocked at how many leaders didn't know their data. That indicated that decisions being made were likely not data-based. I had a skillset many in upper leadership lacked. That was just one reason why I am a star. A few short months into that job, 2020 happened, and the world shut down. When I took the job, I knew I would work four days a week and have every Friday off. On Fridays, I shared information about Cannabis Nursing Solutions™ via email to legislators, people in the cannabis industry, dispensary owners, and anyone I could find on Google. I went to various cannabis events, and once a month, I taught my training course.

2020 was a terrifying time; the unknown concerned me. I did not trust our hospitals to perform in a way that would keep us safe. I didn't want to get Coronavirus, so I worked from home, and my children did virtual school. As I settled into social isolation, I relaxed and realized that I love social isolation! I do my best thinking in quietness.

I didn't notice then, but I had sowed many seeds through reaching out, emailing, and networking. One day, I received a phone call from one of our local senators. I have no idea what email I sent him, but it compelled him to call me and ask about Cannabis Nursing Solutions™. We chatted a bit, and then he referred me to a lobbyist for the Maryland Nurses Association. Her name was Rachel, and we talked for a bit as well. She was delighted to meet me because she didn't know anything about Medical Cannabis. She informed me that a workgroup was being developed to build the guidelines that would support the MD House Bill 617 (2020-MD HB617).

MD HB617 was affectionately called Connor and Raina's Law. The bill allowed children to have access to their medical cannabis at school. The children it was named after were patients with conditions that required them to take medical cannabis daily. Before the bill, they could not take their medicine on school grounds. Their parents had to drive to school in the middle of their workday, take their children off-campus, give them their medicine, and then drive them back to school. In a patient population already experiencing hardship due to their medical condition, that was highly disruptive to the learning process.

I was happy to join the guidelines workgroup. I knew it would change my trajectory. I would meet new people and share my expertise with them. They would support my business, and then, BOOM! Cannabis Nursing Solutions™ would blow up. Since we were smackdab in the middle of a pandemic, we did everything virtually. We met regularly via Zoom.

All of the perspectives on that call were very interesting to me. I was intrigued by the effort that went into creating the guidelines, and I learned how schools used those guidelines to educate our children. It was very informative, and I provided my insights on medical cannabis here and there. My input included general considerations, like the education on the different terpenes. I believe school nurses should be aware of cannabis terpene profiles. Being aware of the terpene profile helps gauge the anticipated effects on the child's body. I am not a school nurse, but generally, as a nurse, I know that I want to be aware of the potential impact of any medication I administer. The school nurse should also be the source of education regarding the plant. She should know, at the very least, plant genetics. Terpene profiles are one aspect of genetics, but there are also cannabinoid profiles. Cannabinoids, like THC, should not be intimidating or scary to discuss with parents, and we should be aware that CBD and THC work together along with the hundreds of other cannabinoids.

I shared some of these ideas during the workgroup and was asked to pull together some safety considerations. I created a reference guide on terpenes for nurses across the state. I had no problem providing this information to them, but I wanted my contributions to be referenced. I did not want them to take my information without acknowledging their source. I was not an employee of the state, and my intellectual property is my intellectual property. When I made that request, it was pushed aside. They were unsure if that was something they could do. There I was again, demonstrating that I was a star.

Then, on another call, there were questions about the authority of the nurse. The questions arose because our Board of Nursing did not participate in many of the meetings. The workgroup compiled a list of questions to ask the Board of Nursing. During the time between the last meeting in that one, they invited the Board of Nursing to answer questions. I don't remember what they asked, but I recall exiting the meeting thinking to myself, "Did they just quote what seems to be the 1960s definition of delegation?" Their responses were outdated. They did not consider the National Council of State Board guidelines. It seemed like this was only done because it was a requirement, not because anyone on that call felt it was necessary. Once the Board of Nursing disconnected, I asked about training the nurses because, at that moment, I knew that the Board of Nursing would not support training.

I was told that training nurses was not something they could consider. After the meeting, I called a lot of people from that workgroup to learn what that meant. I did not receive a clear answer. Based on my understanding of the bill, there was money set aside to facilitate the implementation of these guidelines. When I asked who was responsible, no one knew the answer. Not a big deal. I do not have to be the trainer for all of Maryland's schools. It was okay.

They still wanted to use my content but still refused to reference me. That was the first time I had to demand what I wanted. I had spent a lot of time pulling together the charts and considerations, so I continued to attend the subsequent meetings. After two weeks, someone from the workgroup contacted me. We had a conversation, and then they were able to reference me on the guidelines. Suddenly, they greatly appreciated me and my work and told me often.

I share this story because it is essential to know what advocacy is. Advocacy is moving towards a greater purpose and a more significant cause. Right now, I know that there is a stigma related to medical cannabis. My patients suffer because of the stigma. My representation in that workgroup was for the patients who suffered daily and needed access to their medicine. Yes, I wanted to be able to facilitate the training, but I refused to get lost in my ego. The goal was to ensure that accurate and evidence-based information was available to Maryland Schools so they could implement the proper programs for their Medical Cannabis patients. I did not get lost in my ego, but I never forgot that I am a star.

Part Nine

THE HIEROPHANT

"Walk in your purpose. You are supposed to be here."

The Hierophant is wise, and she understands how to use her wisdom to evoke change. Her keys to life sit before her, and you can see that she's been through some troubling times. Her gown is ripped to shreds, but she is focused with her wand that has turned into a scepter, thoughtfully placed into her hands. People look up to her. They know she brings forth lessons to guide them forward. Her tales were evolutionary, and you need to hear her tales. She cannot be mimicked, so her audience knows they must listen. She is connected and grounded simultaneously, which means she has found balance. She uses her keys to unlock the doors to her next level of collective consciousness. She's ready.

When we step into our true identity, we become a force to be reckoned with. We spend a lot of time in the identities chosen for us, floating through life as if we do not get a choice. Some aspects, such as our gender and race, have been chosen for us. As soon as people see us, they make conclusions based on these two facts alone. The reality is, people don't know anything based on those two facts alone.

When you see me, you see a black woman. This book allowed you to learn about a hero's journey, not just a black woman's journey.

There are 21 basic archetypes, and, at some point, we are all 21. Only nine of the archetypes apply to this journey. We need those archetypes to help us through various points in time. We don't get to choose what is presented to us, but we decide how we approach the lessons. Each archetype comes with lessons we need to master to find balance within ourselves. The journey never looks exactly alike from person to person. This book is to let you know that you, too, are a hero with your own journey. The lessons you learn are unique to you.

In my story, I am a hero who started not knowing who she was, went on a few adventures, and returned ready to transform into The Hierophant. Accepting my role is always challenging for me. In this next phase, I was chosen to be an author.

The experience with the workgroup eventually inspired me to write *Asa's Medicine*. We completed the guidelines in the summer of 2020, but I still had questions about how they would be implemented.

Despite my questions, I went on about my life. I continued offering the Cannabis Nursing Solutions™ training course one Friday a month. I was also acting on an Advocacy Association Board and voted in as Chairman of the Board. I was a member of and even advised on various organizations in the Cannabis Nurse Space. I discovered other Cannabis Nurses and, more specifically, black and brown Cannabis Nurses. Since everything went virtual, that's where I found other people within my niche. I discovered my competitors and learned what they needed. I was making moves, but something was still off. I didn't feel like I was walking in my purpose. I figured the stagnation I felt was because my interaction with the workgroup didn't go as planned. But I also knew that nothing ever goes as planned, so I don't know why I felt so disappointed.

Like I said, after the guidelines were complete, I still had questions. We would implement the guidelines to guide the school systems, which was successful, but what about the social impact? I imagined a child suffering from a chronic disorder finally becoming well enough to attend school because of cannabis and being treated differently by their peers. It's inevitable to be treated differently when you are overtly different. If medical cannabis saves them, why can't they talk about their experience freely in the classroom? How do their friends respond? How would their teacher respond? How does the school nurse know what to say to the child? These questions flew through my mind over and over again. I couldn't help but relate the scenario to my children. What if my daughter goes to school and meets a child who has to take medical cannabis? What would she think? I didn't have answers to my questions, but I couldn't let them go.

One day, I decided to sit outside in my backyard and soak up the summertime sun as I meditated. As I sat there, something told me, "You should write a children's book." I didn't agree with it. I'd never written anything before. My confidence in my writing was in the toilet. Throughout my master's program, my professors always told me that my writing was subpar. I believed it, so I avoided writing. Through my evolution, I realized that if it doesn't make you nervous, it is not worth doing. Writing a book definitely made me nervous, so I decided to do it. At that stage in my life, I was determined to do the opposite of what I normally did, so I wrote *Asa's Medicine.*

I sat outside for about an hour. Once I stood to go back inside, I had written the first draft. I felt pretty good about the first draft. It was everything I was trying to say. It answered all the questions of what the perfect situation would be for Asa. However, I was stuck because I didn't know the next step to take. So, I went to YouTube University. I listened to other authors' stories, challenges, pitfalls, etc.

Writing *Asa's Medicine* tested my confidence in myself. Though I couldn't verbalize it at the time, I had acted on inspired action. I knew that any challenge I experienced related to *Asa's Medicine* was intended to teach me something. So I moved through every obstacle and never hesitated.

The hardest part of the publishing process was finding an illustrator. I had heard so many horror stories about illustrators. I finally found an illustrator in an author group. It was a risky move, but my illustrator did what I asked and created my characters almost the way I imagined them.

One fact I had to let go of was that anybody who contributed to *Asa's Medicine* had to contribute their expertise to the work. So even though the experience wasn't exactly how I imagined, it turned out perfect! I wanted Asa to be a racially ambiguous young boy. I did not want Asa to be stigmatized because of his skin color. I wanted to convey that this could be any of our children. Asa's classroom was diverse. And, of course, Nurse Ashley, another character in the story, was a representative of me.

The illustrator got to work. The details that went into getting *Asa's Medicine* the way it was intended were intense. It was the minor details that got us caught up. Should Asa be smiling or frowning? Should Asa be standing or sitting? We went back and forth, over and over again, to get the illustrations perfect. Finally, we did it! Next was formatting, editing, and finding a self-publishing print-on-demand site. Step after step, I kept going; I didn't question any of it because I knew it was for a larger purpose. However, knowing *Asa's Medicine* was for a larger purpose is different than knowing my larger purpose. During the summer of 2020, we were still amid a pandemic, fighting to accept the brutal details of George Floyd's murder and dealing with riots all over the United States. It was a crazy time.

Many may say that murders happen all the time, and George Floyd's murder was no different than every other murder. As a black woman, I think I've been desensitized by all of the chaos in relation to black men and women. It has become a part of what I know to be a reality. However, George Floyd's murder was a little different, probably because we saw him lay there in agony for such a long time. As a nurse, time moves slow when you're responsible for the next breath of a living body. Watching the video of the officer kneeling on George Floyd's neck for nine minutes and 29 seconds was gut-wrenching. I had flashbacks of moments when I watched the last breath leave another human's body. The lack of remorse on the officer's face as George Floyd took his last breath overwhelmed me with tears. Then, I was back to replaying questions in my head: Who am I? What am I doing here? What is my blackness causing me to feel this way?

Here we go down another rabbit hole. Entrepreneurship taught me that when things affected me personally, they also affected how I did business. It was reflected in how I carried out my daily processes and the messages I communicated to the world. The reality is, being a black woman is a message in and of itself. I realized I needed to understand that message. If I couldn't understand what my blackness meant to me, I couldn't expect the world to understand my blackness.

Instead of writing new content about this topic, I will simply include a speech that I did for the Cannabis Nurses Network Spring Intensive in 2021. It was written during the time of George Floyd before I ever knew that anyone would care about what I had to say.

THE BOXES

A metaphor for the construct

We question our identities by asking who is....Or, who am I?

The answer varies from person to person, and sometimes the answer is relatable, and sometimes it is not, and that is because sometimes we share boxes and sometimes we do not.

So, for the purpose of this talk, I will focus on who Ashley is.

Let's start with the boxes I did not choose but largely shaped my experience in this physical state.

It is the aspects of me most easily identifiable and outwardly projecting.

It is systematized, commodified, and largely underrepresented.

My blackness and my womanhood.

So, if someone asks who I am, at its basic and most fundamental level, I state, "I am a black woman."

... but we all fit into boxes

Sometimes we choose them and sometimes we don't

They are gifts.

Some you can relate to, and others you cannot

Like the mom box ....

They all come with a set of responsibilities that further shape our experiences.

The Nursing Box

I call this a journey which is a series of transitions.

In the beginning, I knew I wanted to work with children.

Decided on pediatrician because of the money I was going to make

How do I get there?

Wanted to do peds nursing but the day I placed a Ngtube in a 9-month-old told me otherwise.

He was sweating, I was sweating

He was crying, I was crying.

That was a no-go for me.

Novice to Expert Journey -In the beginning, you go from having a preceptor and charge nurse to one day being the charge nurse and preceptor. Leadership was never my thing, so I thought.

 I loved pouring into precepts, so I went for my master's in Nursing Education. The master's degree opened doors, and once I got my professional development certification,

I was asked to help support and build a transition to practice program for new graduates- organizational leader.

After a series of events, I somehow moved into Quality and Performance Improvement for a 14-hospital system. Every day, our job was to find ways to make our hospitals run as close to a Toyota car factory as possible. Think about that?

Nonetheless, I was a system leader in a corporate office, and at some point, I wondered, "Why am I here, and where am I going?"

The answer to that has led me to Cannabis Nursing. As we move into the Cannabis Nurse box, we are all actively creating boxes with this box. So here are just a few boxes I've created for myself to play in.

The Author Box is a test of Will, Patience, and

Creation...

Will- can I do something I've never done before? I had to get myself beyond the point of commitment. First is to commit and then take action.

Patience- I had to be patient with myself. Even though I have led and supported large-scale million-dollar projects in the past, this was the longest independent and most personal project I've taken on. The concept of Asa comes from the son we did not get to bear. I had to be patient with myself and those who helped me to create *Asa's Medicine*.

Creation=manifestation. Can my thoughts become the thing?
What is most interesting about Cannabis Nursing is that many of these boxes have only been explored from a surface level which means in every box, there is room for expansion. And, let's be real, if it does not make you nervous, it is not worth doing.

The Entrepreneur Box is a test of flexibility, persistence, and drive.

Flexibility- What Cannabis Nursing Solutions™ started as is not what it is today. And I am okay with it.
Persistence- We have all lived through COVID-19, which has significantly changed the landscape of

how we do business, but I had to keep going.

Drive- Am I going to follow this thing through....
Because it's been hard, but purpose drives action.

The Educator Box

I mentioned earlier that education is my thing, but in this arena, education really looks a lot like advocacy. I have had to pull forward my knowledge of the adult learning principles my understanding of human behavior while being creative in my approach. Another aspect that has made this experience more unique was my need to navigate my own healing. Without the predetermined walls guiding my way, I was lost, and authenticity is not easily found in the midst of hurt and pain. In order to share openly, I had to find healing.

The Leader Box

We are all leaders. Just being interested in a highly stigmatized plant and looking for ways of incorporating it into an antiquated healthcare system makes you a leader. You are doing something that not even half of the nurses in this country are aware of, so for me, if you take one thing you learn today and tell a nurse friend, you are a leader. And with that, I will say this... I am the master of my fate, captain of my soul. I choose the destination for this body, and you do too for yours. And as a collective, we will lead this journey together!

"The highest human act is to inspire."

-Nipsey Hussle

I wrote that speech shortly after I published *Asa's Medicine* in 2021. I was very confused about being in the role of an author. I had to find a way to merge this new aspect with who I had been for most of my adulthood. I knew I was a mom, wife, daughter, nurse ...etc. and had long accepted the responsibility of those roles. However, I didn't feel like the work I put into *Asa's Medicine* deserved the recognition of being called an author. It's a children's book. Writing it was simple, and it only has about 900 words. I felt like real authors wrote books like the one you are reading, and I never thought I could write a book like this.

Early 2021, *Cannabis: The Handbook for Nurses* was released. I was excited when it arrived at my door. It is such a monumental book for nurses; it will likely be the book nursing schools use as a reference. It secures Cannabis Nursing as a specialty even though it has not been identified as such. It talks about the history, cannabinoids, treatment care planning, and more.

I thought the release of that book was exciting, interesting, and disappointing. In my opinion, it is a well-written book, very informative, and necessary for nursing as a collective. However, I don't believe it was written from a well-rounded perspective. It appears that many of the contributors, reviewers, and interviews came from one perspective. I feel as though none of the black nurses contributing to Cannabis Nursing today are represented in that book.

That was disappointing because I am very aware that the people featured in that book will be elevated. When a nursing student opens that book and needs a resource, a reference, or has a question, that nursing student will not find a black or brown nurse to be that resource for them. It reminded me of those history books we got when I was in elementary school. Our history books told the story of Christopher Columbus from a one-sided perspective. They told the story of a man who conquered land with no perspective on those who already inhabited it. This statement is not intended to identify rightness or wrongness. Neither is this statement intended to say that the nurses featured in the book do not belong there. It is intended to say that there are a lot of nurses who could've been elevated with special consideration of the history of cannabis in the U.S.

As I grew in my knowledge of what blackness meant to other people besides myself, I realized my behavior was an act of complacency. I allowed current constructs to thrive because I didn't speak up. Whenever I walked into a room and allowed people to cipher information from me that was not protected, I acted complacently.

I also realize that the term "War on Drugs" wasn't just a set of words; they were arsenal. When people talk about the war on drugs, they talk about it as if they are "woke." As long as they mention the war on drugs, they are aware of the impact and the trickle-down effect it had on a large group of people. Black people make up 14% of the population. This means 14% of the population has likely been affected directly or indirectly by the War on Drugs. That includes my friends and family. Some of the stagnation that exists in communities is directly connected to the history of this country.

As you can see, I did not experience stagnation, but it breaks my heart that so many people around me have experienced it. If I allowed my heart to break every day, it could. So, the disappointment about that book runs deep for me, but I prioritize the collective nurse thought over the collective black thought because that's the system we live within.

Although I choose to prioritize the nurse collective, I do not choose to ignore who I am. When I arrive, I arrive as I am. The more I experience in life, the more archetypes I experience, the more I get to know the innermost me. Each experience allows me to peel back the layers of who I was and look forward to who I am. The more I do that, the more I attract to me. This is the key to unlocking the door to my wisdom.

Words that we say daily get watered down because of their repetitiveness. An example of this is the term "War on Drugs." The term was powerful until it was not. When I walk into a room, I choose to use more intentional words intended to foster change in awareness. As my audience's awareness grows, it is my responsibility to take my awareness to the next paradigm. I mentioned earlier that I was a professional job starter. That was not the case. I am a professional paradigm shifter.

Once I made this shift, I began to stand out. The disappointing realities should not be why I cannot speak my truth. Maybe I always stood out and didn't realize it before. My journey made apparent that I was attracting miraculous things to me. Although the handbook did not feature black or brown nurses, this black nurse has a larger purpose and will elevate herself as she moves as an Endocannabinoid Specialty ™ Nurse.

I find it funny when magical things happen that we never call magic. I had a magical experience recently, and she probably did not realize how magical it was for me. One day, I woke up and went about my day as normal. I was speaking about my anxieties related to making the world aware of *Asa's Medicine*, and a publicist offered to help me, pro bono. She was able to secure me and my book to be featured in High Times, Outlaw Report, and more.

And the magic just continued to happen. Shortly after that, a doctor reached out to me, and we co-published an article that was featured in First Time Parent. I was featured in various podcasts. I was asked to be on a panel at the Cannabis Science Conference, and our topic was "A Revolution in Healthcare." I was given a spotlight section for the Maryland Nurses Association convention, educating Maryland nurses about medical cannabis in our state. I also spoke at the American Public Health Association Conference. *Asa's Medicine* has been to conferences across the country, conferences I've never even attended. It can also be found in Maryland Dispensaries across the state of Maryland. The release of *Asa's Medicine* opened doors for me.

So, heroes or survivors? For a long time, I was just surviving. I was unable to see the power I held within myself. I let the world happen to me repeatedly and for far too long. Then, I realized I was a hero on a journey called life. The true question is: Am I a hero or survivor?

My answer?

It depends on how you look at it.

ABOUT THE AUTHOR

Ashley Wynn-Grimes MS, RN is the Founder of Cannabis Nursing Solutions™ and author of children's book *Asa's Medicine.* In 2021, Ashley was honored as Baltimore Business Journal Leaders in Health Care. Native to Baltimore, MD, Wynn-Grimes, a Black female entrepreneur and widely respected medical professional, is dedicated to empowering patients and nursing professionals on cannabinoid therapy options with impactful educational medical programs that also serve to promote diverse representation and medical equality in healthcare.

ABOUT CANNABIS NURSING SOLUTIONS™

OUR VISION

To shift the perspectives in healthcare by empowering healthcare providers to become change agents through solutions that are inclusive of spiritual, mental and holistic healing practices.

OUR MISSION

To provide awareness of the evolution of healthcare through books and speaking engagements; while providing healthcare providers with the support they need through training, coaching, networking, and various opportunities to achieve their personal and entrepreneurial goals.

This allows us to....

Offer a distinct service that utilizes the Nursing Process, Individualized Treatment Care Plans, and a method of evaluating progress in the continuum of care for our patients. We provide strategies to patients seeking alternative and holistic solutions to manage chronic illness. We will educate, empower and assist you on your journey to safely utilize medical cannabis to bring you back to oneness. Through education and support of spiritual, mental, physical, and social processes, Cannabis Nursing Solutions™ is an advocate for natural, integrative healing philosophies which includes the consumption of cannabis for medicinal purposes. Simply put... *we make cannabis easy!*

OUR VALUE STATEMENT

Cannabis Nursing Solutions™ has 7 core values which employees are to implement in conducting business practice. These core values consist of spirituality, wellness, empowerment, expansion, learning, transformation and inclusivity of human's perception of the world!

Spirituality We know that there is a greater presence then what we perceive.

Wellness We know that wellness is a spectrum and achieving wellness is a continuous journey.

Empowerment We know that everyone participates in wellness and we should all be empowered to do what is in the best interest of the patients and the professionals that support them.

Expansion We know that each individual experiences an expansive journey. Healthcare providers continue to grow in their knowledge and expertise so they can be of the highest service to the patients they serve.

Learning We know that in order to expand we must be willing to receive information and determine best fit for application.

Transformation We know that transformation is a fluid process and a product of human development.

Inclusivity We accept all perspectives and realize that inclusivity is more than a construct but a respect for all perspective across all spectrums of the human experience.

For more information about Cannabis Nursing Solutions™ visit www.cannabisnursingsolutions.com.

THANKS FOR YOUR SUPPORT!

Writing and publishing a book is no easy feat. However, my efforts would be fruitless if no one purchased or supported. I want to thank you, the reader, for purchasing and reading this book. I hope that this book provides you with the push you need to create your own magic in this big world. Also, I want to give a special thanks to the **first 100 people** who preordered this book. Your continued support means the world to me!

THANK YOU!

Your Endocannbinoid Specialty Professional,
Ashley Wynn-Grimes

CONNECT WITH THE AUTHOR

Thank you for reading, *STIGMATIZED*. Ashley can't wait to connect with you! Here are a few ways you can contact the author. You can also scan the QR Code below with your mobile device to connect with the author.

WEBSITE   CANNABISNURSINGSOLUTIONSLLC.COM
INSTAGRAM   CANNABISNURSINGSOLUTIONS
FACEBOOK   CANNANURSINGSOLUTIONS
LINKEDIN   ASHLEY THE CANNABIS NURSE
EMAIL
GRATITUDE@CANNABISNURSINGSOLUTIONSLLC.COM

Made in the USA
Middletown, DE
22 September 2022